Cambridge Elements ≡

Elements in Shakespeare and Text
edited by
Claire M. L. Bourne
The Pennsylvania State University
Rory Loughnane
University of Kent

SHAKESPEARE, MALONE AND THE PROBLEMS OF CHRONOLOGY

Tiffany Stern
The Shakespeare Institute, University of Birmingham

CAMBRIDGE
UNIVERSITY PRESS

CAMBRIDGE
UNIVERSITY PRESS

Shaftesbury Road, Cambridge CB2 8EA, United Kingdom

One Liberty Plaza, 20th Floor, New York, NY 10006, USA

477 Williamstown Road, Port Melbourne, VIC 3207, Australia

314–321, 3rd Floor, Plot 3, Splendor Forum, Jasola District Centre,
New Delhi – 110025, India

103 Penang Road, #05–06/07, Visioncrest Commercial, Singapore 238467

Cambridge University Press is part of Cambridge University Press & Assessment,
a department of the University of Cambridge.

We share the University's mission to contribute to society through the pursuit of
education, learning and research at the highest international levels of excellence.

www.cambridge.org
Information on this title: www.cambridge.org/9781009224727

DOI: 10.1017/9781009224710

First published 2023

A catalogue record for this publication is available from the British Library.

ISBN 978-1-009-22472-7 Paperback
ISSN 2754-4257 (online)
ISSN 2754-4249 (print)

Shakespeare, Malone and the Problems of Chronology

Elements in Shakespeare and Text

DOI: 10.1017/9781009224710
First published online: March 2023

Tiffany Stern
The Shakespeare Institute, University of Birmingham

Author for correspondence: Tiffany Stern, t.stern@bham.ac.uk

ABSTRACT: In 1778, Edmond Malone published his first contribution to Shakespeare scholarship, *An Attempt to Ascertain the Order in Which the Plays Attributed to Shakspeare Were Written*. He revised and republished it in 1790 and began a further revision of it which was printed posthumously in 1821. This Element is about the three versions of Malone's *Attempt* and the way they created, shaped, focused, directed and misdirected our idea of the chronology and sequence of Shakespeare's plays. By showing Malone's impressive, fallible choices, adopted or adapted by later editors, it reveals how current Shakespeare editions are, in good and bad ways, Malonian at heart.

This Element also has a video abstract: www.cambridge.org/stern

KEYWORDS: Malone, chronology, Shakespeare, Shakespeare's sequence, eighteenth-century editing

ISBNs: 9781009224727 (PB), 9781009224710 (OC)
ISSNs: 2754-4257 (online), 2754-4249 (print)

Contents

1 Introduction

The order in which Shakespeare wrote his plays – which work he wrote first, which last and how his technical and imaginative skills developed over time – has long been a subject of intense interest. But few clues survive as to what that sequence was. Only in the eighteenth century, over 150 years after Shakespeare had died, did Edmond Malone (1741–1812) come up with a way of collecting and combining external and internal information about the plays to create a date order (or 'chronology') for Shakespeare's texts. We have been using Malone's chronological methodology, and often his results, ever since.

This Element tells two interconnected stories. One is about Malone's brilliant creation of a Shakespeare chronology, and his three attempts – published in 1778, 1790 and 1821 – to settle the order of Shakespeare's plays. The other is about chronology now, as reflected in single volumes and complete works, and how it descends, methodologically, from Malone. In revealing how current Shakespeare editions still adopt and adapt Malone's impressive, fallible choices, it suggests that Malone's problems, irrespective of the analytical tools used or order proposed, remain ours: we are asking a question that does not admit of a single answer – when was a play *written*? – and often placing in one sequence plays dated by very different kinds of evidence, external and internal, though the surviving texts may have other date ranges entirely.

This Element is for anyone wondering when plays were written (and what that question means); anyone interested in the extraordinary story that brought Shakespeare's chronology into being; and anyone who finds liberating the notion of chronological instability.

It was in 1776 that Edmond Malone, an Irish lawyer keen to become a literary scholar, went to visit the famous Shakespeare editor George Steevens. Malone had produced notes and a brief biography for the forthcoming *Poems and Plays* of Oliver Goldsmith (published in 1777); he hoped to be asked to do something similar for the Shakespeare edition that Steevens was preparing. Steevens did indeed invite Malone to help him, presumably expecting a contribution of the 'Goldsmith' variety: a handful of useful scholarly notes, together with a 'safe' and earnest biography.

But though Malone was to provide copious notes to be added into the Johnson–Steevens Shakespeare (so-called as Steevens' edition was an update of Samuel Johnson's), he was unable to find enough new material to make up a Shakespeare biography, noting that 'very few particulars have been recovered, respecting [Shakespeare's] private life, or literary history'.[1] Hungry for a research project that would make a genuine editorial contribution, Malone realised that there was evidence yet to be gathered and catalogued about the performance and publication of Shakespeare's plays. Collecting and analysing such information would enable him to establish a Shakespeare chronology which would show when and how Shakespeare's 'genius' (a very eighteenth-century concept) emerged and flourished. The result would be a biography, but of Shakespeare's mind, rather than his life. This would have the advantage, too, of answering the question that had haunted so many editors – how did Shakespeare turn into *Shakespeare*: 'what was the first Essay of a Fancy like *Shakespear's*?' asked Nicholas Rowe in 1709; 'when [was] every piece . . . composed, and [was it] writ for the Town or the Court', wondered Alexander Pope in 1725; by what 'gradations of improvement', enquired Samuel Johnson in 1765, did Shakespeare proceed?[2] So closely linked was *An Attempt to Ascertain the Order in Which the Plays Attributed to Shakspeare Were Written* to biography itself that when Malone's executor, James Boswell the Younger, published the final, posthumous, version of the chronology in 1821, he made it section XV of Malone's lifelong and never-to-be finished research project, his *Life of Shakespeare*.

Malone did not cease his work on the chronology after he published *An Attempt to Ascertain the Order in Which the Plays Attributed to Shakspeare Were Written* (in volume one of the Johnson–Steevens ten-volume *Plays of William Shakespeare* of 1778). Concerned above all with accuracy, and refreshingly ready to confront the notion that his own conclusions might

---

[1] Edmond Malone, *An Attempt to Ascertain the Order in Which the Plays Attributed to Shakspeare Were Written* in William Shakespeare, *The Plays*, ed. Samuel Johnson and George Steevens, 10 vols (1778), 1: 270. [Hereafter *Attempt* (1778)].

[2] William Shakespeare, *The Works*, ed. Nicholas Rowe, 6 vols (1709), 1: vi; William Shakespeare, *The Works*, ed. Alexander Pope, 6 vols (1725), 1: vii; William Shakespeare, *The Plays*, ed. Samuel Johnson, 8 vols (1765), 1: xxxix.

be wrong, Malone reworked his *Attempt* to reflect his new thoughts and later discoveries; he was partway through the third version of it when he died. The three versions of 1778, 1790 and (posthumously) 1821 indicate that establishing a Shakespeare chronology ultimately bracketed and defined everything else that Malone achieved in Shakespeare scholarship.

That there are three different versions of *Attempt* also reveals the careful way Malone approached and reapproached his subject: he never thought his work complete and did not view any of his chronologies as fixed. Indeed, in all three of his editions, he is careful to point out that his conclusions are contingent, dependent on the facts he has to hand, and that he is ready to 'transfer ... credit' if a scholar with a 'superior degree of antiquarian sagacity' is able to update and improve his work.[3] And he was true to his word: he accepted one of Edward Capell's ideas – that 'the sweat' in *Measure for Measure* might refer to the 1603 outbreak of plague – though he added that 'it is the only [observation ...] which in the smallest degree could throw any light on the present inquiry into the date of our author's plays'.[4] Here, as he grudgingly takes on a Capell notion, he shows how his ultimate priority is to let what he sees as 'evidence' triumph.

As well as gathering and ordering material for Shakespeare's chronology, Malone also invented a way of writing about it. Shakespeare scholarship was, at the time, fractious, ardent, opinionated and often mischievous. For instance, the editor with whom Malone was so impatient to work, George Steevens, had attributed all explanatory notes about Shakespeare's bawdy to a couple of vicars who annoyed him: his Hampstead neighbour, the Reverend Richard Amner, and a divine with whom he had had a quarrel, the Reverend John Collins.[5] By contrast, Malone had no impish side: he introduced into Shakespeare scholarship his rigorous and lawyerly

---

[3] *Attempt* (1778), 346.

[4] Edward Capell, 'The Plays' Order and Date' in *Notes and Various Readings to Shakespeare*, 3 vols (1779–80), 2: 34; *Attempt*, in William Shakespeare, *The Plays and Poems*, ed. Edmond Malone, 10 vols (1790), 1: 346. [Hereafter *Attempt* (1790)].

[5] See Marcus Walsh, 'George Steevens and the 1778 Variorum: a Hermeneutics and a Social Economy of Annotation', in *Shakespeare and the Eighteenth Century*, ed. Peter Sabor and Paul Yachnin (Aldershot: Ashgate, 2008), 71–83.

pedantry. That is obvious even in his book's awkward and overlong title, *An Attempt to Ascertain* . . . . 'Attempt' ('for so he has modestly styled it', notes a reviewer in 1783) frankly acknowledges that the work to come is less than a 'discovery' or a 'proof'; it is a first (and second, and third) try at categorising a topic 'on which conviction cannot at this day be obtained'.[6]

At around the same time that Malone was diligently gathering and organising facts for his chronology, English Romanticism was staking impassioned claims for Shakespeare's boundless imagination. Malone's thorough, detailed and documentary-rich analyses infuriated poets such as Samuel Taylor Coleridge, whose diary mockingly dubs him 'the Genitive Plural of a Greek Adjective'. ('Malon' means 'more'; the genitive plural never changes: Malone's copious work was unchangingly tedious.) 'Malone', continued Coleridge, was

> that eternal Bricker-up of Shakspeare – Registers, Memorandum Books, and Bill, Jack, and Harry, Tom, Walter, & Gregory, Charles, Dick, and Jim &c &c lived at that time, but that nothing more is known of them – but of the importance when half a dozen Players' Wills can be made to stretch thro' half a hundred or more of pages – tho' not one word in them that by any force can be made to illustrate either the times or life or writings of Shakspere, or indeed of any time.[7]

What is interesting, though, is that Coleridge was not against the idea of a Shakespeare chronology. On the contrary, he wanted an order for Shakespeare's plays for the same reason that Malone did: he yearned for insights into his hero's literary development. He did, however, have his own ideas about how that development might be traced. Coleridge's rival

---

[6] Anon, 'Capell's Notes and Various Readings of Shakespeare', *The Critical Review*, 56 ed. Tobias Smollett (1783), 401–9 (405); *Attempt* (1778), 346; repeated in 1790 and 1821.

[7] Samuel Taylor Coleridge, *The Notebooks*, ed. Kathleen Coburn, 5 vols in 10 (New York: Pantheon Books, 1973), 3: 3277.

chronology – he was ultimately to come up with four of them – witheringly rejected Malone's 'data' in favour of what he called 'internal evidence', but which was in fact his opinion.[8] Dividing Shakespeare's work into five 'aeras' (eras), he explained how the first, and earliest, contained Shakespeare's experiments with different forms of drama, and consisted of *Love's Labour's Lost*, *Pericles*, *The Winter's Tale*, *Cymbeline*, *Titus Andronicus*, *The Comedy of Errors*, *All's Well that Ends Well*, *The Taming of the Shrew*, *A Midsummer Night's Dream*, *Much Ado About Nothing* and *Romeo and Juliet*.[9] For him, then, it was Shakespeare's imagined experiments with dramatic form that was the bedrock for the writing to follow. The Malone–Coleridge division between fact and imagination typified, and helped secure, the rift between scholarly Shakespearean documentation and passionate interpretation that has continued to this day. But it is notable that Coleridge, as much as Malone, needed a chronology to shape his Shakespeare thoughts, and intriguing that he constructed his very different sequence from what he also understood to be internal evidence. The extent to which discovering and analysing internal evidence can be an act of interpretation is an issue that this Element will explore in some detail.

It was, however, Malone's *Attempt* that was to set the standard for scholarly chronology. Reviewers of the period recognised the impressive and field-defining nature of Malone's research, while also hinting at its tedious quality. So *The Monthly Review* paid homage to Malone's 'elaborate enquiry', while *The Critical Review* found 'This "Attempt" ... extremely dry, and full of black-letter erudition'.[10] James Boswell the Younger, who spent years completing the twenty-one-volume posthumous *Plays and Poems of William Shakspeare* for Malone, extolled his predecessor's 'accurate knowledge', 'unwearied research' and 'inflexible adherence to truth',

---

[8] Samuel Taylor Coleridge, *Shakespeare Criticism: Marginalia, Lectures, and other Notes from Coleridge's Manuscripts*, ed. Thomas Middleton Raysor, 2 vols (London: Constable, 1930), 1: 209.

[9] Coleridge, *Shakespearean Criticism*, 2: 213.

[10] Anon, 'The Plays of William Shakspeare', *Monthly Review*, 62 (1780), 12–26 (19); Anon, 'The Plays and Poems of William Shakspeare', *The Critical Review* 3 ed. Tobias Smollett (1791), 361–9 (364).

while acknowledging that the scholar did not have 'the pointed vivacity of Mr Steevens's manner', and could come across as 'too minute and circumstantial in collateral details'.[11] Malone cultivated 'the figure of the magisterial historian in possession of superior knowledge', observes Richard W. Schoch; it was, and indeed is, the very dullness of Malone's writing, the heftiness of its factual load, that has often made his work and methods seem unimpeachable.[12] Malone's authoritative way of writing became the way in which chronology and theatre history (two fields he effectively invented) were written: even now, the 'factual' bits of early modern scholarship still sometimes adopt the superior, hectoring tone of a leading barrister that descends from Malone.

Given that Malone created the scholarly subfield of Shakespeare's chronology, found the documents for it, invented the way in which they are discussed and codified a method for ordering plays that we still broadly use, it is hardly surprising that current chronologies follow, roughly, his sequence. Yet *Attempt* is often unfairly represented in modern scholarship. Malone's least-grounded surmises and most surprising play dates, generally taken from the first version of *Attempt*, are sometimes supplied as though they represent his only thoughts on the subject: few who write about Malone's *Attempt* acknowledge how carefully he reworked it throughout his life, how impressively ready he was to publish retractions of his earlier opinions and how bound we still are to his conclusions.

The dates that Malone came up with for his first, second and third *Attempt* are shown in Table 1 so that his surprising and less surprising decisions, as well as his changes of mind, can be seen. The table is shown against the most recent complete works to have come out, the revised Bate and Rasmussen *RSC Shakespeare* (2022) – so that the three *Attempts* can be compared to an example of recent if unsystematic current thinking (important chronologies by Wiggins with Richardson, and Taylor and

---

[11] James Boswell, *A Biographical Memoir of the Late Edmond Malone, Esq* (London: Nichols, Son, and Bentley, 1813), 13.

[12] Richard W. Schoch, 'Edmond Malone and the Search for Theatrical Intelligence', in *Writing the History of the British Stage, 1660–1900* (Cambridge: Cambridge University Press, 2018), 290.

Table 1 Malone's dates per *Attempt*; RSC *Complete Works* dates

Play	Malone 1 1778	Malone 2 1790	Malone 3 1821	RSC 2022
Shrew	1606	1594	1596	1589–92
2 Henry VI (contention)	1592*	1591*	1591*	1591
3 Henry VI (true tragedy)	1592*	1591*	1591*	1591
Two Gentlemen	1593	1595	1591*	1591–2
Titus	1589*			1591–2; perhaps revised 1594
1 Henry VI	1591*	1589	1589	1592
Richard III	1597	1597	1593*	1592 or 1594
Errors	1596	1593*	1592*	1594
LLL	1591	1594*	1594*	1595
Dream	1595*	1592	1594*	1595–6
Romeo	1595*	1595*	1596*	1595–6
Richard II	1597*	1597*	1593*	1595–6
John	1596*	1596*	1596*	1595–7

Table 1 (cont.)

Play	Malone 1 1778	Malone 2 1790	Malone 3 1821	RSC 2022
Merchant	1598*	1598*	1594*	1596–7
1 Henry IV	1597*	1597*	1597*	1596–7
2 Henry IV	1598*	1598*	1598*	1597–8
Much Ado	1600*	1600*	1600*	1598
Henry V	1599*	1599*	1599*	1599
As You Like It	1600*	1600*	1599*	1599
Caesar	1607	1607	1607	1599
Hamlet	1596	1596	1600*	1600–1
Merry Wives	1601*	1601*	1601*	1600–1 (revision of text of 1597–9?)
Twelfth Night	1614	1614	1607	1601
Troilus	1602*	1602*	1602*	1601–2
Othello	1611	1611	1604*	1604
Measure	1603*	1603*	1603*	1604
All's Well	1598	1598	1606*	1605
Timon	1610	1609	1610	1605
Lear	1605*	1605*	1605*	1605–6

Macbeth	1606*	1606*	1606*	1606
Antony	1608*	1608*	1608*	1606–7
Coriolanus	1609*	1609*	1610*	1608
Pericles	1592			1608
Cymbeline	1604	1605	1609*	1610
Winter's Tale	1594	1604	1611*	1611
Tempest	1612*	1612*	1611*	1611
Henry VIII	1601	1601	1603 (rev 1612*)	1613

Loughnane, which supply date ranges rather than single dates, will be addressed later in this Element).[13] An asterisk demarcates a Malone date that is within two years of the RSC's; as shown, by the final *Attempt* that is thirty-one of thirty-six plays. (NB: As Malone believed that *Titus Andronicus* and *Pericles* were not fully Shakespearean, he left them out of his second and third versions of *Attempt*; *Two Noble Kinsmen* never featured on any of his lists.)

The sections that follow explore Malone's thoughts and rethoughts as he came up with his first *Attempt* for the Johnson–Steevens *Plays of William Shakspeare* (1778); his second, revised, *Attempt*, for the prolegomena to his own edition of the *Plays and Poems of William Shakspeare* (1790); and his third, semi-revised *Attempt* (he was hampered by failing eyesight and died before he completed his revision) for his posthumous edition of the *Plays and Poems of William Shakspeare*, completed by James Boswell the Younger (1821). Looking at the dilemmas Malone faced in marrying external and internal evidence, and in creating a single chronology from fusing the two, this study argues that to understand Malone's three versions of *Attempt* is to understand why and how he and, as a consequence, we have been asking an unanswerable question and drawing conflicting conclusions ever since.

Section 2 is on the way Malone sourced and catalogued information from publication and court records, often for the first time. It details how remarkable his gathering and pooling of material was, but reveals, too, the sometimes subjective way in which he analysed it. The section also touches on the fundamental problem with external evidence, namely, that it supplies a date by which a version of the work already exists, rather than what Malone wanted to know: when it was written.

Section 3 looks at what Malone did to date plays for which external information was not available: gather information from within texts, such as literary cross references, and potentially datable words, objects, people and events. Showing how Malone had to force, and sometimes invent, dates for lexical or historical habits, it calls attention to the assumptions that Malone made to shore up his 'discoveries', in particular, that Shakespeare's fictions

---

[13] William Shakespeare, *Complete Works*, ed. Jonathan Bate and Eric Rasmussen (2nd ed., London: Bloomsbury Academic, 2022), 2456–60.

regularly referred to factual contemporary events, including those in his own life. Very few of Malone's internal proofs, it suggests, stand up to scrutiny. Arguing that rare datable internal information often comes from 'before' or 'after' when Malone dates the play, it raises questions about using internal information for chronology at all.

Section 4 considers the story told by internal information in the collected works of Shakespeare published after his death, the 'First Folio', and ignored or downplayed by Malone: signs that most Folio-only Shakespeare texts had been revised for the Blackfriars theatre, and/or new musical requirements, and/or the page, and are therefore internally 'late'. This study argues that Malone's desire to find 'early' chronological indicators made him ignore facts that, as a consequence, have not been consistently taken into account since: that texts in the Folio tend to have a date range that extends from during to beyond Shakespeare's lifetime; and that many and perhaps all Folio texts date, at least in certain respects, from the 1620s.

Section 5 is on the central difficulty besetting Malone's chronology: that he made one single chronology from conjoining external and internal information. Explaining that the order in which Shakespeare *wrote* his plays and the *dates of extant texts* are not the same, it suggests that any single chronology that dates some plays from external and some from internal information cannot be correct. It traces the fused single chronology back to the question Malone chose to ask: when were the plays of Shakespeare written? As plays were written and rewritten over different periods of time, internal information is bound to yield more than one date at which a text was (re)composed, while external information, when present, bears witness only to a single performance of the work, in a version that may well no longer be extant, and sometimes never existed as a textual property. A single chronology thus muddles work and text.

Section 6, on current practice, looks at how many of Malone's methods – and therefore problems – we have adopted. Several important recent chronologies have, for exciting reasons, redated or rethought the sequence of individual Shakespeare plays; they are also alert to questions of adaptation. Yet editions are still asking Malone's undefined question about when the plays were written, often provide Malone's actual examples, and are only selectively alert to 'late' internal Folio dates. Any complete works published in 'chronological order' follows Malone's mingling of external and internal information to create one chronology and puts into a sequence texts that may, in the form in which they survive, be far apart in date.

The conclusion suggests that a two-part chronology – that separates external from internal evidence and draws attention to chronological instability – is a safer alternative that will also celebrate, rather than obscure, chronological instability.

2 External Information

The most secure dates that Malone could find for the plays of Shakespeare came from external information: information, that is to say, from sources beyond the content of the surviving texts. Some of this information was supplied by plays printed in Shakespeare's lifetime: quartos (books made up of sheets folded into four) or octavos (books made up of sheets folded into eight). Their detailed title pages, designed to market their contents in a wide variety of ways, might supply such external information as the name of the company that put on the play, the name of a theatre where the play was performed or the occasion on which the play was put on for royalty. Another source of external information was the large volume of complete plays of Shakespeare published in 1623, seven years after its author's death, and often known these days as the 'First Folio' (though technically, 'Folio' is the title for any large book made up of sheets of paper that are folded just once). The preliminary matter to Shakespeare's First Folio includes dedications that make references to productions; a list of some, but not all, of the major actors who had performed in the plays; and promotional poems that gave occasional details about staging and place.

In a world before well-stocked public libraries, the very act of finding (nearly) all of Shakespeare's printed texts in order to acquire the information listed above was itself an enormous achievement. The British Museum, founded in 1753, was able to provide Malone with only a few original Shakespeare texts; and the Bodleian Library in Oxford not only lacked many Shakespeare quartos but had also sold on its First Folio in favour of a later one (its original Folio was only to be repurchased by the library in

1906). Indeed, the Bodleian's excellent current Shakespeare collection is largely Malone's, whose books were donated to that institution by his brother, Richard Malone, Lord Sunderlin. In his own time, Malone had to get his information about Shakespeare's printed texts by consulting his friends' books, borrowing what he was able and seeking and buying such early modern quartos as he could find.[14]

Beyond playbook title pages, Malone had to hunt widely for Shakespeare documents at a time when even identifying where to look, yet alone what to look for, was tricky. Wrote Malone's early biographer, James Prior:

> Manuscripts, wherever found, were carefully consulted; no expense or application was spared to exhume something like truth and substance out of the graveyards of time. Collectors, antiquaries, and college men, whose lives had been spent in storing their shelves or their memories with knowledge of the past, were solicited to disburse such acquisitions as could be turned to account.[15]

Confronted with a wide range of different kinds of information, manuscript and print, easy to access and difficult, Malone favoured the kinds of records that, as a lawyer, he most valued: reliable public accounts and legal documents. For obvious reasons, he relished most highly those records that came with dates, gravitating, then, towards written sources and away from 'alternative histories' as Schoch points out.[16] De Grazia notes that Malone's choice to avoid what he deemed untrustworthy – chatty anecdotes and inherited memories – means that crucial information that he might have recovered has been irrevocably lost.[17]

---

[14] See Peter Martin, *Edmond Malone, Shakespearean Scholar* (Cambridge: Cambridge University Press, 1995), 21.

[15] James Prior, *Life of Edmond Malone* (London: Smith, Elder, & Company, 1860), 49–50.

[16] Schoch, 'Edmond Malone and the Search for Theatrical Intelligence', 266.

[17] Margreta de Grazia, *Shakespeare Verbatim: The Reproduction of Authenticity and the 1790 Apparatus* (Oxford: Clarendon Press, 1991), 50–1.

Through his assiduous documentary research, however, Malone was able not just to acquire but also to catalogue for the first time a range of types of external evidence. The material he extracted from the title pages of quartos, for instance, he combined with information supplied by the Stationers' Register (SR): the book – actually books – in which early modern publishers recorded their ownership of texts prior to publication.[18] By joining information from the SR with quarto and octavo title pages, Malone was able to observe, for the first time, crucial publishing oddities, which remain a puzzle today. There were, for instance, plays that had been entered in the SR but not printed (or, just possibly, printed and then lost), like *Antony and Cleopatra* (SR 1608) and *As You Like It* (SR 1600). Conversely, there were texts that had been printed but had not been entered into the SR, like *Love's Labour's Lost* (1598) and *Romeo and Juliet* (1597). By conjoining what quartos and the SR told him, Malone produced a singular achievement in its own right, the first ever detailed account of Shakespeare's publication history, simply as an aspect of determining chronology.

However, as it was the order in which Shakespeare's plays were *written* that Malone had set out to determine, he had to guess back from the relatively solid information he had about date of publication to the date of writing. This obliged him first to conjecture how long before publication performance must have taken place, and then how long before performance writing must have happened. Malone concluded that Shakespeare's plays were unlikely to make it to the SR 'till they had been some time in possession of the stage', a reasonable, but not infallible, rule of thumb.[19] (Masque texts, for instance, were often printed before or on the day of performance, to be read alongside the production.[20]) Though Malone also

---

[18] Recently transcribed and published by George Steevens as 'Extracts of Entries on the Books of the Stationers' Company', in which he had noted all entries relevant to Shakespeare in William Shakespeare, *Plays*, ed. Johnson and Steevens, 10 vols (1778), 1: 253–68.

[19] *Attempt* (1778), 289.

[20] The publication of masque texts for performance is discussed in Peter Walls, *Music in the English Courtly Masque, 1604–1640* (Oxford: Oxford University Press, 1996), 20.

observed exceptions – *Much Ado*, printed in 1600, he decided was also 'written . . . early in the year 1600' for reasons that will be addressed later – his general unspoken 'rule', extracted from the conclusions he draws, seems to have been that the first performance of a play was roughly two years before publication and followed hotly upon writing.[21]

On occasion, however, though Malone trusted the publication records, he nevertheless dismissed the dates that they gave him. He had originally dated *Comedy of Errors* to 1596, 'because the translation of the *Menaechmi* of Plautus, from which the plot appears to have been taken, was not published till 1595'.[22] By the second *Attempt*, he had acquired additional external information – from which, these days, the play is dated – that there had been a performance of *Comedy of Errors* at Gray's Inn in December 1594. He was not convinced, however, that *The Comedy of Errors* performed there was definitely Shakespeare's play; and he found the date unsatisfactory either way, as he strongly felt that Shakespeare's play exhibited 'internal proofs of having been one of Shakespeare's earliest productions'.[23] He continued, therefore, to worry about the late (1595) date for the publication of Shakespeare's source, the translation of *Menaechmi*, and concluded that Shakespeare must have read the translation in manuscript, before it had even been licensed for print in the SR. So, in the second *Attempt*, Malone dated *Errors* 1593, and then, in the third *Attempt*, 1592.[24] Given that *Menaechmi* had circulated in manuscript before publication – the printer explains in his 1595 dedication that the translator originally 'Englished' the text 'for the use and delight of his private friends' – Malone's ever earlier choice of years does have a rationale.[25] But his rationale presents problems of its own, for though Shakespeare *could* in principle have read any text in manuscript well before publication, the logical extension of the argument makes the SR useful only as a, sometimes distant, supplier of '*terminus ad quem*' or end dates (a problem Malone had to wrestle with again for different

---

[21] *Attempt* (1778), 306ff. [22] *Attempt* (1790), 289. [23] *Attempt* (1790), 290, 289.

[24] *Attempt* (1790), 289; *Attempt,* in William Shakespeare, *Plays and Poems,* ed. James Boswell and Edmond Malone, 21 vols (London: F. C. and J. Rivington et al., 1821), 2: 324. [Hereafter *Attempt* (1821)].

[25] W[illiam] W[arner], *Menaecmi* (1595), A3r.

reasons when dating *Two Gentlemen*, as will be addressed). It would have been easier for Malone had he been prepared to allow Shakespeare enough Latin to read the play himself without a translation. As it was, however, in each iteration of *Attempt* Shakespeare is said to have read the source manuscript for *Errors* even earlier, meaning that the date of the play itself becomes harder and harder to establish: if the source was available to Shakespeare in manuscript two or three years before publication, why not four or five or six?

At other times, Malone trusted the dates provided by the SR, but, on weighing the evidence, reinterpreted the meaning of the information so conveyed. So he, following Steevens, had initially thought that the SR's 1594 entry for a lost (or never printed) book, *A Wynter Nyghts Pastime*, was to Shakespeare's *Winter's Tale* under an earlier title; as a result, he had dated the play, in the first *Attempt*, to 1594.[26] By the second *Attempt*, however, a 'more attentive examination of the play' – and the sense he was developing about the nature of Shakespeare's literary progression (he noted the text's paucity of a habit he thought typical of early work, rhyming couplets) – made him believe that *Winter's Tale* came from a much later date: he shifted it to 1604 and, in the third *Attempt*, to 1611.[27] He did so by rejecting the notion that *Wynter Nyght's Pastime* had anything to do with Shakespeare. In fact, as no copies of *A Wynter Nyght's Pastime* survive, it is not possible to know what relationship it may or may not have borne to *Winter's Tale*. What can be said is that Malone's identification of a potential early Shakespeare text, and his later rejection of it, while reflecting his thoughtful attempt to reconcile information with observation, are ultimately dependent on the sophisticated, but subjective, ideas he was forming concerning the nature of Shakespeare's development.

A different source of external information was court performance. Malone had access to a manuscript put together by the antiquary George Vertue, who had transcribed the contents of Lord Harrington of Stanhope's 'Accounts of the Treasurer of the Chamber' of 1613. These Vertue/Stanhope accounts

---

[26] George Steevens had published the SR entry for '*a Winter Nyghts Pastime*' in his 'Extracts of Entries' (1778), 1: 255.

[27] *Attempt* (1790), 349.

supplied the names of the plays that had been put on at court in 1613 as part of the lead-up to the nuptials of Frederick V, Elector Palatine and Princess Elizabeth Stuart: *Much Ado, The Tempest, Winter's Tale,* '*Sir John Falstafe*' (potentially *1* or *2 Henry IV* or *Merry Wives*), *Othello, Caesar's Tragedy* (probably, but not certainly, *Julius Caesar*), and, in a separate entry, *The Hotspur* (*1 Henry IV*), and *Benedicte and Betteris* (*Much Ado* again).[28] The 1613 record, though, only provided distant end dates: it gave the date by which a play must already have been in existence, but did not directly supply information about when it had been written. The 1613 records did, however, provide other useful information: that a Shakespeare play might be performed under a variety of titles, and that plays might be revived long after they had first been written and performed – Malone more often took the former into account than the latter.

Other information about court performances reached Malone late in life, and only entered the last version of *Attempt*. So, in the 1821 *Attempt*, he redates *Othello* from 1611 (first and second *Attempt*) because 'We know [. . . it] was acted in 1604'.[29] Boswell, who edits and completes Malone's final *Attempt*, does not have a source for the redating of this play, and footnotes 'Mr. Malone never expresses himself at random. I therefore lament deeply that I have not been able to discover upon what evidence he *knew* this important and decisive fact.'[30] A bit of paper in one of Malone's scrapbooks in the Bodleian Library, now called the 'Malone Scrap', however, supplies the answer: it provides the contents of a 1604–5 court Revels Account in which court performances of *Measure for Measure, Comedy of Errors, Merchant of Venice, Othello, Merry*

---

[28] George Vertue's transcription is lost, but the documents themselves are reproduced in the Folger Shakespeare Library, 'Shakespeare Documented', https://shakespearedocumented.folger.edu/resource/document/codex-chartaceus-1612-1613-expenses-including-those-performances-plays-shakespeare [accessed 17 July 2022]. For more on the complicated history of the George Vertue notes, see Ivan Lupić, 'Shakespeare, Cardenio, and the Vertue Manuscripts', *Ars & Humanitas*, 5 (2010), 74–91. As *Much Ado About Nothing* is here listed by two different names, it is impossible to know whether *Sir John Falstafe* is the same as, or a different play from, *The Hotspur*.

[29] *Attempt* (1821), 404. [30] *Attempt* (1821), 404.

Wives, *Love's Labour's Lost* and *Henry V* are all recorded. This 'Malone Scrap',
thought to be in the hand of Malone's friend Sir William Musgrave – who as
Commissioner of the Audit Office Board had access to the historic Revels
documents – supplies Malone with new end dates for all the plays mentioned,
including the new early date for *Othello*.[31] The way Malone uses this new
information also reveals his working processes. Though from the 'Malone
Scrap' and its details of the Revels Account he now knew that most plays
performed in 1604–5 at court were revivals (i.e., he already knew of their
existence pre-1604), he did not therefore conclude that *Othello* had been written
earlier than 1604. Rather, as 1604 is the earliest date he can conceive of for a play
he had hitherto assumed to be much later, he placed it in that year, perhaps
correctly (the company would then be performing one new play and several
'old' ones at court), though once again, his personal judgement was shaping the
way he assessed the information he had acquired. As it seems, when Malone
had, as with publication records, to guess back from the date of performance to
the date of writing, he tended to conclude that the *first record* of a court
performance was the *record* of a *first* performance – rather than a single instance
of performance within the stage life of a play.

   Another major external source that Malone came by late, only in time for
the third *Attempt*, was the *Office Book* of Henry Herbert, who had been

---

[31] The 1604–5 revels documents, together with another of 1611–12, were first
published by Peter Cunningham as *Extracts from the Accounts of the Revels at
Court* (London: The Shakespeare Society, 1842). And, as the drunken
Cunningham later tried to sell the purloined accounts themselves to the British
Library, and as their discovery had been heralded and supported by noted forger
John Payne Collier, the records have at various times been thought to be
forgeries. It was indeed the discovery of the 'Malone Scrap' that suggested that
these texts had been transcribed, pre-Cunningham, by Musgrave and so are
probably genuine – though S. A. Tannenbaum, *Shakespeare Forgeries in the
Revels Accounts* (New York: Columbia University Press, 1928), and
C. C. Stopes, *The Seventeenth Century Accounts of the Masters of the Revels*
(London: Oxford University Press, 1922) concluded that the 'Scrap' itself was
forged. The whole story is related in Arthur Freeman and Janet Ing Freeman,
John Payne Collier: Scholarship and Forgery in the Nineteenth Century, 2 vols (New
Haven: Yale University Press, 2004), 1: 406–10.

acting and then actual Master of the Revels (responsible for overseeing court festivities, and for censoring plays before performance) from 1623 to 1673. That manuscript, discovered in 1787 mouldering in a chest at Ribbesford Manor, Worcestershire – where Herbert had once lived – supplied details about what the job of being Master of the Revels entailed. Malone borrowed the book (now lost, though fragments and partial transcriptions remain), which revealed how plays of the period were censored, licensed and prepared for court. It even enabled him to find a date for *Winter's Tale* that fitted his sense of the surviving text. He learned, from the office book, that Henry Herbert had had to relicense *Winter's Tale* in 1623 because the original manuscript of the play had been lost; and he learned too that the original, lost text had been licensed for the stage by the earlier Master of the Revels, George Buc. As Buc had the reversionary grant of the office of Master of the Revels in 1603 but did not come fully into 'possession of his [Master of the Revels] place [until] August, 1610', he redated *Winter's Tale* to just after Buc's formal accession, 1611 (though he could, from this information, have dated it both earlier and later, of course).[32] Malone had also, by the final *Attempt*, gained access to Philip Henslowe's *Diary* which supplied financial details about the Rose Playhouse in the 1590s and later. That book was important for his theatre historical work, but he did not use it for his *Attempt*, presumably because the plays that it mentioned, *Titus Andronicus* and *1 Henry VI*, were texts that he no longer thought were significantly by Shakespeare.

Some external information that Malone obtained came from published texts. This included Francis Meres' *Palladis Tamia* of 1598, a book which set out to show that English playwrights were every bit as good as classical writers.[33] In the process of writing a 'comparative discourse of our English Poets, with the Greeke, Latine, and Italian Poets', Meres provided lists of what he judged to be 'excellent' modern plays, including twelve by Shakespeare: six comedies (*Two Gentlemen of Verona, The Comedy of Errors, Love's Labour's Lost, Love Labour's Won, A Midsummer's Night*

---

[32] *Attempt* (1821), 463.

[33] Malone had been alerted to this text by Thomas Tyrwhitt in his *Observations and Conjectures upon Some Passages of Shakespeare* (1766)], 15.

Dream and *Merchant of Venice*) and six tragedies (*Richard II, Richard III, Henry the IV, King John, Titus Andronicus* and *Romeo and Juliet*).[34] Assuming '*Henry the IV*' is *1 Henry IV*, Meres' *Palladis Tamia* thus supplies an end date, 1598, for eleven known plays plus the elusive *Love's Labour's Won*, which Malone first thought to be *All's Well that Ends Well* under a different title, and later stopped attributing (it is now sometimes said to be one of Shakespeare's known comedies under another title; sometimes said to be a lost play).[35] Though Meres did not name all the Shakespeare texts Malone thought were in existence by this time – *The Taming of the Shrew* and *2* and *3 Henry VI* are not mentioned in his account – Malone nevertheless used absence from Meres' list to date other plays.[36] He maintained, for instance, that *Much Ado* cannot have been extant by 1598, as Meres did not include it. In fact, however, the play might have been extant but Meres did not know about it; or did know but did not choose to refer to it. A third alternative is that it might have been performed that year but only after Meres' book had been completed: *Palladis Tamia* was entered onto the SR on 7 September 1598, and in principle a new Shakespeare play might have been mounted later that year.[37] Tyrwhitt's researches also supplied Malone with some more clearly datable 'one off' pieces of information, like the passage in Robert Greene's *Greenes, groats-vvorth of witte*, published in 1592, which derides 'Shake-scene' for having a '*Tygers hart wrapt in a Players*

---

[34] Francis Meres, *Palladis tamia* (1598), 2O2r. As Malone can be vague or inconsistent with transcription, here, as elsewhere, titles and quotations are supplied from actual early modern texts, rather than Malone's transcription of them, though with i/j and u/v regularised.

[35] A fragment from the 1603 account book of Christopher Hunt, a stationer, detailing amongst his list of plays for sale *loves labor won*, indicates that a play was published with that name, but not what it was. The fragment was found in a binding in 1953. See Folger Shakespeare Library, 'Shakespeare Documented', https://shakespearedocumented.folger.edu/resource/document/loves-labors-won-listed-fragment-stationers-account-book [accessed 17 July 2022].

[36] *Attempt* (1790), 293.

[37] All references to the Stationers Register are quoted from Edward Arber ed., *A Transcript of the Registers of the Company of Stationers of London*, 5 vols (London: Privately printed, 1875–84), 3: 125.

hyde'; this is a parody of a line in *3 Henry VI*, 'Oh Tygres Heart, wrapt in a Womans Hide' (TLN 603), and gives a terminal date for that play too.[38]

Some external sources in published texts were, Malone came to think, false friends. Thus Malone had first dated *Hamlet* to 1596 because he knew of Thomas Lodge's description, published that year, of 'the Vizard of ye ghost which cried so miserally [sic] at ye Theator . . . *Hamlet, revenge*'.[39] He was, however, uncomfortable with the earliness of the reference, noting of Shakespeare's actual text that 'the general air of [the play] has not . . . the appearance of an early composition'.[40] When he later learned of an even earlier reference to *Hamlet*, in Thomas Nashe's 1589 preface to Robert Greene's *Menaphon*, he came up with a different explanation for all these early reports. Deciding that Shakespeare's actual *Hamlet* could be dated to 1600 through its internal references to 'translated Tasso' (the first translation of Torquato Tasso, *Godfrey of Bulloigne, or The recouerie of Ierusalem*, by Edward Fairfax, had appeared in 1600) and its account of the 'inhibition of the players' (the playhouses too had been closed in 1600), he decided that the other reports were about a previous, non-Shakespearean version of the play.[41] He noted that most Shakespeare plays were based 'on the performances of preceding writers', a continuation of an observation Steevens had made in a footnote to Malone's discussion on *Macbeth* that 'a time may arrive, in which it will become evident from books and manuscripts yet undiscovered and unexamined, that *Shakespeare* never attempted a play on any argument, till the effect of the same story, or at least the ruling incidents in it, had been tried on the stage, and familiarised to his audience'.[42]

Malone concluded that these references to an earlier *Hamlet* were to the source-play 'on which . . . [Shakespeare's] tragedy was formed'.[43] He even attempted to identify the author of this pre-Shakespearean

---

[38] Thomas Tyrwhitt supplied the Greene reference – Robert Greene, *Greenes, groats-vvorth of witte* (1592), F1v – in a note to George Steevens; see S. Schoenbaum, *Shakespeare's Lives* (Oxford: Clarendon Press, 1971), 114.

[39] Thomas Lodge, *Wits Miserie* (1596), 56.

[40] *Attempt* (1778), 292. He was writing of quarto of 1604 and the Folio of 1623; *Hamlet* Quarto 1 of 1603 was not discovered in his lifetime.

[41] *Attempt* (1821), 370. [42] *Attempt* (1778), 328. [43] *Attempt* (1821), 371.

Hamlet.[44] Thomas Nashe had called the *Hamlet* author a 'Noverint', so Malone, bearing in mind that 'ancient deeds ... frequently began with the words *Noverint Universi*', concluded that the original writer had been a deed-writer or scrivener; Nashe had also described the style of that play as 'English *Seneca*', so Malone determined the writer was classically influenced. As the playwright Thomas Kyd was a scrivener in his father's footsteps and a classically inspired writer, Malone proposed Kyd as the author of the earlier (now often called after the German term), '*Ur*'-*Hamlet*.[45] Thus Malone studiously hunted down evidence to confirm what he already believed, brilliantly using forensic analysis to argue away information that was in itself trustworthy but still, to him, seemed wrong against his assessment of play's general 'air'.

The interpretation of another piece of external evidence about *Hamlet* reflected Malone's changing relationship to George Steevens. A marginal annotation written in manuscript by Gabriel Harvey onto a copy of Thomas Speght's *Chaucer* included the following: 'The younger sort takes much delight in Shakespeares Venus, & Adonis: but his Lucrece, & his tragedie of Hamlet, Prince of Denmarke, have it in them, to please the wiser sort.'[46] Malone initially thought that this note had been penned in 1598; that would have supplied a terminal date for Shakespeare's play. But that belief, he later claimed, resulted from the 'loose manner' in which Steevens had described the marginalia to him. When Malone himself consulted the *Chaucer* and read the marginalia, he determined that 'the note in question may have been written in the latter end of the year 1600'; it thus helped confirm the later date he was now giving the play.[47] That particular piece of marginalia has continued to be a frustrating source: it is not itself dated, so coming up with a date for it requires dating all the other marginalia in the book and then deciding whether or not they were all written in the same year. What is intriguing here is that Malone and Steevens were now fighting for 'ownership' of Shakespeare, and

---

[44] Robert Greene, *Menaphon* (1589), **3r.   [45] *Attempt* (1821), 371–2.

[46] Folger Shakespeare Library, 'Shakespeare Documented', https://shakespearedo cumented.folger.edu/resource/document/manuscript-marginalia-gabriel-harvey-refers-hamlet-lucrece-and-venus-and-adonis [accessed 17 July 2022].

[47] *Attempt* (1821), 369.

that Malone's feelings about Steevens' trustworthiness, as well as his desire to secure a later date for *Hamlet*, inspired his redating of the marginalia that supplied his source. Private friendship – or the reverse – had a serious effect on how facts were recorded, conveyed and interpreted and hence what they were or might mean.

Malone's subjectivity with respect to external documents was nowhere clearer than when his sense of Shakespeare's biography – the very thing he was trying to discover – took over. For instance, he knew from two sources (a Henry Wotton letter, and Edmund Howe's 1618 manuscript addition to John Stow's *Annals*) that there had been a fire at the Globe playhouse in 1613 while a new play about Henry VIII had been in performance under the title *All Is True*. But, like Samuel Johnson, Malone thought that Shakespeare's *Henry VIII* was in origin an early text, written to flatter Elizabeth I 'at a time when the subject must have been highly pleasing', and that what survived was therefore an updated revision rather than a new play: for Shakespeare would 'have . . . thrown [Elizabeth] into the back-ground', he maintained, if writing a play from scratch in the time of James I.[48] He dated *Henry VIII* to 1601 in the first two *Attempt*s and to 1603 in the third. That idea has not had much traction since, but it shows how Malone's sympathies – here about what he imagines Shakespeare's attitude to royalty to have been – could affect the way he reasoned through the information he discovered.[49]

As the above shows, external information, no matter how trustworthy, could never tell Malone when Shakespeare *wrote* the plays. Indeed, that is not in the nature of external information, which is always about plays

---

[48] *Attempt* (1821), 388; 390. He presumably did not know of Samuel Rowley's *When you see me, you know me* (1605), another play of James' time about Henry VIII.

[49] Recently Wiggins in his entry on *All Is True* in Martin Wiggins, in association with Catherine Richardson, *British Drama: a Catalogue*, 9 vols to date (Oxford: Oxford University Press, 2015), 6: 231, has argued that John Webster imitated the text in his *White Devil* (perf 1611–12) and that therefore the later 1613 performance may have been a revival. Gary Taylor and Rory Loughnane are not convinced by the parallels that Wiggins cites, 'The Canon and Chronology of Shakespeare's Works', in *The New Oxford Shakespeare: Authorship Companion* ed. Gary Taylor and Gabriel Egan (Oxford: Oxford University Press, 2017), 587–8.

already in existence – being entered in the SR, or published, or put on at court, or seen or read by contemporaries. And while this section has illustrated how cautiously and thoughtfully Malone gathered and analysed, and reanalysed, and further gathered, his documentary evidence, it has equally shown how interpretative Malone had to be with seemingly straightforward evidence, sometimes questioning the validity of the information itself, and sometimes its relationship to a Shakespeare play. He was repeatedly guided too by friends, enemies and his instincts – good ones, but not therefore right – as well as fact.

3 Internal Information

Malone did not know of all the early play printings, quartos and octavos, which we now do. As far as he was concerned, there were twenty-one plays that had not been 'printed in our author's lifetime':

> *King Henry VI. P. 1.*, The Second and Third Parts of *K. Henry VI.* (as he wrote them) *The Comedy of Errors, The Taming of the Shrew, The Two Gentlemen of Verona, King John, All's Well that Ends Well, As you like it, King Henry VIII. Measure for Measure, The Winter's Tale, Cymbeline, Macbeth, Julius Caesar, Antony and Cleopatra, Timon of Athens, Coriolanus, Othello, The Tempest*, and *Twelfth Night.*[50]

He therefore had to come up with dates for when these works were written, most of which (the exceptions being *2* and *3 Henry VI*, printed in quarto and octavo in highly variant versions in 1594 and 1595, the authorship of which Malone doubted; and *Othello*, printed in quarto in 1622) had not been printed until the Folio of 1623. For the eighteen Folio-only texts, there was virtually no external information. So, as Steevens put it admiringly

---

[50] *Attempt* (1790), 264. Some quartos were not to be discovered at all until after Malone's death, including *Hamlet* Q1 (1603), *Titus Andronicus* Q1 (1594), and *1 Henry IV* Q0 (1598).

(at a point when he liked him), Malone hunted out 'such internal evidence as the pieces themselves supply'; or, as Malone himself explained, he found evidence from inside Shakespeare's 'several dramas' themselves.[51] Internal evidence – cross references within texts to contemporary published works or recent historical and/or bibliographical events, or the use of modish words – enabled him to supply dates for the plays for which he lacked other information and to refine the dates for the plays for which he had only external (and so terminal) dates.

The strongest kind of internal evidence that Malone could find was direct reference to other printed literature, which had the added advantage of, usually, providing a year of publication. Unfortunately for Malone, the most unambiguous internal references were to sources, which, though often easy to identify, had come into existence before the plays based on them, and thus supplied little of use to a chronologer. That goes for major history play source texts like Raphael Holinshed's *Chronicles* (1577; rev. 1587), and the 'classical' history source text, Thomas North's translation of *Plutarch* (1579, rev. 1595, rev. 1603). Just occasionally, however, he found sources that might be useful for dating. Malone's notion that Shakespeare came to North while writing *Macbeth* (because he thought 'My *Genius* is rebuk'd, as ... *Mark Antonies* was by *Caesar*' [TLN 1046] was an allusion to Plutarch's *Life of Antony*) enabled him to conclude that Shakespeare was reading the latest, 1603, version of that book and so provided a '*terminus a quo*' (initial date) for the work.[52]

More useful publications and manuscripts, in dating terms, were those written during Shakespeare's playwriting life and cross-referenced in his texts. These include accounts of the shipwreck of Sir George Sommers on Bermuda in 1609 (recorded in two pamphlets of 1610), which supplied Malone with an initial date for *The Tempest*, and Samuel Harsnett's *Declaration of Egregious Popish Impostures* (1603), which, with its demon names of Frateretto, Fliberdigibbet, Maho and Modu, gives an initial date

---

[51] Steevens, 'Extracts of Entries' (1778), 1: 268; *Attempt* (1778), 272.

[52] *Attempt* (1790), 366. First Folio quotations are taken from the Norton Facsimile prepared by Charlton Hinman (New York: Norton, 1968), using the through-line-numbers (TLN) of that edition, but regulating i/j and u/v.

for the sections of *King Lear* in which 'poor Tom' uses the same terms.[53]
Even these instances, however, required Malone to rely upon dates supplied
by the SR and publication (though, as shown in Section 2, he suggested that
manuscripts might circulate for years before reaching publication and could
have earlier dates entirely).

Sometimes, a direct and datable reference hindered Malone. In *Two
Gentlemen of Verona*, there are two references to the classical characters
Hero and Leander: this initially made Malone think that Shakespeare had
been influenced by Marlowe's poem *Hero and Leander*. That was fine for him
when, in the second *Attempt*, he was dating *Two Gentlemen of Verona* to
1595, for Marlowe's *Hero and Leander* had entered into the SR in 1593 (and
he assumed, incorrectly, had been first published shortly thereafter). But
when, in the third *Attempt*, he revised the date of *Two Gentlemen of Verona*
back to 1591, he had therefore to conclude – as with the source to *The
Comedy of Errors* – that Shakespeare had been influenced by Marlowe's
poem pre-publication. He suggested 'Shakespeare might yet have read this
poem before the author's death in 1593', though he confusingly went on, 'a
piece left by [Marlowe] for publication was probably handed about in
manuscript among his theatrical acquaintances'.[54] This argument requires
Marlowe to be alive, on the one hand, circulating his manuscripts 'before . . .
death'; on the other, leaving a piece for publication (while alive? in his
will?) which then travels in theatrical circles.[55] As manuscripts did circulate
pre-publication, he may be right; but Malone is using special pleading to

---

[53] Shakespeare, *Plays*, ed. Boswell and Malone (1821), 15: 381–3; *Attempt* (1778),
322.

[54] *Attempt* (1790), 299; *Attempt* (1821), 320.

[55] The poem *is* thought to have circulated pre-publication, and Shakespeare, whose
Venus and Adonis could be seen as a matching epyllion, may have read it for that
reason (though for him to have done so in 1591 is still a stretch). András Kiséry
maintains that *Hero and Leander*'s circulation will have been in the inns of court
and John Wolfe's bookshop after Malowe's death: see 'Companionate
Publishing, Literary Publics, and the Wit of Epyllia: the Early Success of *Hero
and Leander*', in *Christopher Marlowe, Theatrical Commerce and the Book Trade*, ed.
Kirk Melnikoff and Roslyn Knutson (Cambridge: Cambridge University Press,
2018), 178–9.

downplay a seeming fact offered by internal information that no longer suits his notions (oddly, he did not conclude that a reference to this well-known story could be made without access to Marlowe's text at all).

Other internal cross references required him to make judgement calls as to whether Shakespeare was the originator or imitator of a shared passage. When Malone, prompted by Steevens, saw that lines from The tragedie of Darius (1603), by William Alexander, first Earl of Stirling, resembled a section of *The Tempest*, he decided that 'one author must ... have been indebted to the other'.[56] His conclusion, that 'Shakspeare ... borrowed from Lord Sterline [sic]', reflected and helped substantiate external information he had acquired that suggested that *The Tempest* was a late play. In a parallel instance, however, he drew the opposite conclusion: in the knowledge that Sterling had written a play on the subject of *Julius Caesar* and published it in 1607, he suggested that Shakespeare's play must date from later than Lord Sterling's, as 'no contemporary writer' would have been 'daring enough to enter into the lists with [Shakespeare]'.[57] Here, Malone decides whether Sterling is imitated (*Tempest*) or imitator (*Julius Caesar*) depending on which argument best fits the date he has already chosen.

Generally, Malone preferred to think that Shakespeare influenced, rather than was influenced by, other poets. When spotting a parallel between *Macbeth* and George Chapman's *The Tragedie of Caesar and Pompey* (1607), he speculated that the author of *Caesar and Pompey* 'had Macbeth's soliloquy in view'; this helped him date Shakespeare's play to pre-1607.[58] Of course, it is to be expected that Shakespeare both imitated and was imitated, but it is revealing to see how even definite allusions require interpretation and, in the jostle for priority, are in danger of, at the very least, supplying reversible dates.

Other problems with internal literary references include the question of whether they are even there. As with Sterling, Malone regularly found allusions to the work of Samuel Daniel in Shakespeare: but to what extent is that because he had read Sterling and Daniel? In the second and third versions of *Attempt*, for instance, he compares Samuel Daniel's line 'Death

---

[56] *Attempt* (1778), 343. [57] *Attempt* (1821), 445. [58] *Attempt* (1778), 324.

dallying seekes, / To entertaine it selfe in Loves sweet place', from *The Complaynt of Rosamond* (1594), with 'Shall I beleeve / That unsubstantiall death is amorous' (TLN 2956), from *Romeo and Juliet*.[59] But both Daniel and Shakespeare seem to be making a routine death/sex parallel using different language; the similarity between the two, based on sentiment, not poetry, may be coincidence. Malone, who could only analyse what he had read, habitually discovered Shakespeare comparisons in the books he knew best. On occasion, he may have imposed, rather than extracted, the parallels he drew.

A difficulty of Malone's creation is revealed by his mixed response to Vincentio Saviolo's guide to duelling, *Vincentio Saviolo His Practise in Two Bookes* (1595). From the second *Attempt* onwards, Malone maintains that Shakespeare's duelling terminology comes from Saviolo, though there are, of course, other, non-textual ways to learn such vocabulary. Yet, though Malone uses Saviolo to help date *Romeo and Juliet*, stating that that text's reference to '*the first and second cause*' indicates writing 'after the publication of Saviolo's Book', he cannot do likewise when he meets the same phrase in *Love's Labour's Lost*.[60] For 'first and second cause', 'passado' and 'duello', all terms used by Don Armado in that text, he spots 'Saviolo's treatise', but has to conclude that Shakespeare's 'passage . . . may have been an addition'. This is because he believes *Love's Labour's Lost* to be Shakespeare's 'first *original* dramatick production' and is dating that play to 1594.[61] The very book that helps him date one play hinders him in dating another, and, once more, he has in the case of *Love's Labour's Lost* to argue around the very external information that he has worked so hard to find.

His notion that a definite allusion may supply a date only for a passage, rather than the play, is a striking acknowledgement that Shakespeare's texts must have been augmented over time. But that fact raises fundamental questions about using internal information to date entire texts *at all*. If an internal reference dates a passage, rather than the text, then cannot that be said of all cross references? And if the datable line may be a revision, then all

---

[59] Samuel Daniel, *Delia and Rosamond Augmented* (1594), H1v; *Attempt* (1790), 302; repeated 1821.

[60] *Attempt* (1790), 347. [61] *Attempt* (1790), 326–9.

internal information, even when datable, can potentially be dismissed as later in origin (or, as with the *Hero and Leander* reference, earlier in origin) than the rest of the text. Follow through that line of argument and no internal information, even when secure, can ever date more than itself: a fragment may well have a different date from that nebulous term 'the play'.

Malone had equal problems with the non-literary internal information that he found, particularly when he put pressure upon single words. Inspired by his friendship with the lexicographer and Shakespeare editor Samuel Johnson, he tried to use early modern words to date the texts that employed them; the difficulty was that there was at the time no record of 'first recorded usage', meaning that words themselves were notoriously hard to fix in time. He was the first to point out that 'equivocation' in *Macbeth* was a word that had been repeatedly used in the 1606 Gunpowder Plot trial of Henry Garnet, the English Jesuit priest hanged drawn and quartered for equivocating and lying: he dates *Macbeth* to 1606 partly as a result.[62] Using the same logic, in the first two iterations of *Attempt*, he dated *Twelfth Night* to 1614 from the line 'if you be an undertaker, I am for you', which, he believed (following advice from Thomas Tyrwhitt), was a topical reference to the so-called 'parliamentary undertakers' managing elections in that year.[63] He later, however, changed his mind about 'undertaker', which he now felt had been 'used in a . . . general sense, without the particular allusion', and redated *Twelfth Night* to 1607.[64] He did not similarly reconsider 'equivocation', however, and did not redate *Macbeth*. That is not to say that he should have done so or that either date is wrong; but it is to point out that any lexically based date is dependent on whether the word in question is being used in a specific or general sense, and if it is tellingly current to a particular moment or is, or becomes, a term in regular use.

---

[62] *Attempt* (1821), 409.

[63] Discussed in Arthur Sherbo, *Shakespeare's Midwives: Some Neglected Shakespeareans* (Delaware: University of Delaware Press, 1992), 37.

[64] *Attempt* (1821), 442.

A different form of topical information avidly researched by Malone, but more troubling in dating terms than ever, was social and environmental history. He thought he saw in the *As You Like It* line 'I will weepe for nothing, like *Diana* in the Fountaine' (TLN 2062–3), a reference to the fountain of Diana by The Cross in Cheapside, mentioned by John Stow in his *Survey of London* (1598), where it is described as having 'Thames water, prilling from her breasts'.[65] But the Stow reference to water spraying from nipples is at odds with the Shakespeare reference to water seeping from eyes; whichever, if any, of the country's Diana statues this line refers to, it is almost certainly *not* the Cheapside one. Yet Malone excitedly repeated his Diana–Cheapside observation in the second and third *Attempt*. That is because, by the second edition of Stow's *Survey of London*, published in 1603, the reference to the effigy of Diana in the Cheapside fountain had been updated: the statue was 'now decayed'.[66] Malone could then use the degradation of the Cheapside 'Diana' to confine the date of *As You Like It* to the period between the two Stow editions, that is, between 1598 and 1603. As 1600 is also when *As You Like It* is listed in the SR, the statue's decay bolsters the documentary reference and vice versa.[67] But here a researched allusion that apparently confirms the text's date is doing the reverse: if a different weeping Diana fountain *were* to be identified – the famous one at Nonsuch provides just one such example – then the internal references would have to be redated accordingly.[68]

A constant trouble with social history was that it tended not to supply dates at all. Malone often identified facts but had to force them to yield dates in ways open to question. He used Mistress Quickly's observation in *Merry Wives* that 'coach after coach' filled with knights came to see Mistress Ford

---

[65] John Stow, *A Suruay of London* (1598), 252.

[66] John Stow, *A Suruay of London* (1603), 269. [67] *Attempt* (1790), 327.

[68] The famous Diana fountain in the Diana Grove at Nonsuch Palace was constructed earlier, in the 1580s; it too seems to have had water spraying from the breast and is thus a parallel to the Cheapside effigy rather than Shakespeare's. See Martin Biddle, 'The Gardens of Nonsuch', *Garden History* 27 (1999), 145–83. There need, of course, be no actual source: Diana fountains at the time were something of a cliché.

to date the Folio text to around 1605, as 'coaches', he observed, did not come into general use until that year.[69] However, the quarto text of 1602 describes Nym as Pistol's 'Coach-fellow', so Malone's information is not as definitive as he thinks.[70] Similarly, Malone first dated *Coriolanus* to 1609, but was troubled by Volumnia's exhortation to her son to address the people 'humble as the ripest mulberry'. Observing that King James had brought a forest of mulberry trees to England in 1609 – they were supposed to encourage the silk trade, as silkworms feed on mulberries – he worried about the 'ripe' observation, which implied Shakespeare had seen 'some of the fruit in a state of maturity before he wrote *Coriolanus*'. His first conclusion was that 'some *few* mulberry-trees ... had been ... planted before [1609]'.[71] Later, concerned that he had allowed his belief about the date of a play to challenge his historical information, he solved the issue by redating *Coriolanus* to 1610, so giving Shakespeare the chance to see a ripe mulberry and 'history' the upper hand. Had he but known it, mulberry trees had long been planted before King James' errant mission (James planted the wrong kind of mulberry to kickstart the silk industry). Mulberries, like equivocation, undertakers, statues and coaches, are not as obviously datable as Malone had hoped.[72]

On the few occasions when topical allusions were – perhaps – to datable events, it is not always clear to which. Malone believed that mentions of 'plague' or 'pestilence' were specific references to the great plague of 1593, which affects his dating of *Romeo and Juliet* and *Two Gentlemen of Verona* (articulated in the second *Attempt*), while the plague of 1603 affects his dating of *Measure for Measure*.[73] These could, however, be general references to the plague, which lived on in memory even when there was not an

---

[69] *Attempt* (1790), 329.

[70] William Shakespeare, *A Most Pleasaunt and Excellent Conceited Comedie, of Syr Lohn Falstaffe, and the Merrie Wiues of Windsor* (1602), C2v.

[71] *Attempt* (1790), 118; 376.

[72] For evidence of mulberry trees in England from the Roman period onwards, see Morus Londinium, 'Timeline of the Mulberry Tree in London', https//www.moruslondinium.org/research/timeline [accessed 17 July 2022].

[73] *Attempt* (1821), 349; *Attempt* (1790), 299; *Attempt* (1821), 385.

epidemic. Likewise, so sure was he by the third *Attempt* about Shakespeare's interest in Henri IV of France that he thought *Merchant of Venice*'s reference to 'the flourish, when true subjects bowe / To a new crowned Monarch' (TLN 1392–3) was *about* Henri IV 'crowned at Chartres in the midst of his *true* subjects in 1594', and that *Comedy of Errors*' 'arm'd and reverted, making warre against her heire' (TLN 914–15), was 'an allusion ... to King Henry IV. the *heir* of France': he redated both plays as a result.[74] But while references to plagues, or coronations, or wars, or indeed heirs, *might* be about particular datable instances, they might equally be general or fictional references, not tied to real events at all.

Sometimes Malone questioned or rethought the dates that he had drawn from history; sometimes he did not. 'Some to the warres, to try their fortune there; / Some, to discover Islands farre away' (TLN 310–11) was a line that, in the second *Attempt*, made him date *Two Gentlemen of Verona* to 1595, as he thought it a reference to the Spanish threat to England in that year and Raleigh's voyage to Trinidad and Guiana.[75] By the third *Attempt*, however, he felt 'that these circumstances by no means establish the date I had assigned to this play', because they could equally refer to Essex's earlier trip to France and Raleigh's previous voyage.[76] As this brave change of mind shows, however, Malone's tendency was always to think internal references were topical in some way: he did not readily embrace the notion that they might be entirely fictional. On the contrary, his need for facts of this kind obliged him to believe that Shakespeare regularly referred to events from the time when he was writing: 'Shakspeare is fond of alluding to events occurring at the time when he wrote'; 'our author ... has frequent allusions to the circumstances of the day'.[77] As his proof of Shakespeare's allusions was generally the very instances he was adducing, however, all such arguments are circular.

A further allusion Malone found to an actual event was to an unusual seismic happening in Shakespeare's childhood. He had, at first, strongly rejected Tyrrwhitt's idea that the Nurse in *Romeo and Juliet* is referring to the English earthquake of 1580 when she recalls "Tis since the Earth-quake now eleven yeares' (TLN 376–7). He found it 'improbable, that

---

[74] *Attempt* (1821), 332; *Attempt* (1790), 288. [75] *Attempt* (1790), 298.
[76] *Attempt* (1821), 320. [77] *Attempt* (1821), 331; 384.

Shakspeare ... should have adverted, with such precision, to the date of an earthquake ... felt in his youth' and asked why, anyway, Shakespeare would make an English earthquake take place in Verona.[78] But he later had a change of heart, partly because he had now subsumed his own notion that Shakespeare made frequent allusions to the events of his own time. He decided that the Nurse *was* in fact referring to the English earthquake of 1580, which therefore dated the play to eleven years from that reference, 1591 (he did not mention that, if Shakespeare was concerned with accuracy of this kind, he would have had to rewrite the line on a yearly basis; or that this kind of precision was unusual for an era in which people were not always sure about their own ages). More awkward for Malone was the fact that, by this point, he had decided that the play dated to later, 1595 (because, as discussed earlier in this section, of its references to 'the first and second cause', which he traced to Saviolo); by the final *Attempt* he had dated the play 1596.[79] So he was obliged to conclude that 'Shakespeare might have laid the foundation of this play in 1591 and finished it at a subsequent period': an observation much to his credit, in that retaining his earlier rejection of the earthquake as a dating device would have saved him from a 'fact' he no longer wanted.[80] But his dating of a single passage to four and, later, five years before he dates 'the play' raises further questions that query the whole approach of *Attempt*. Yes, *Romeo and Juliet* may have been written piecemeal, over a five-year period, but so may every other play; accepting this argument makes dating any play and so determining 'the order in which the plays of Shakespeare were written' impossible, particularly given that other passages, as have been shown, have been said to be later than the date of their play. What this 'solution' reveals, once again, is that a whole play cannot be dated from a single topical allusion: not only because that allusion dates only one passage but also because plays are not necessarily written in one single year. Take that to its natural conclusion and the entire *Attempt* is shown to be fundamentally misguided. If a play may be written over five years and then, later, revised, how can 'the date' on which it was written ever work as a subject for enquiry?

---

[78] *Attempt* (1778), 290. [79] *Attempt* (1790), 301; *Attempt* (1821), 344.
[80] *Attempt* (1790), 303–4.

Connections Malone drew between Shakespeare's age and stage are a particularly awkward extension of his hunt for identifiable moments of 'history': for they make Shakespeare's plays into the biography they were supposed to determine. Examples include the notion that *Romeo and Juliet* is an early play because it has 'a story ... likely to captivate a young poet', though Shakespeare, throughout his life, wrote plays that feature young people in love, such as *Winter's Tale* and *The Tempest*; and the idea that Lady Constance's grief for the death of Arthur in *King John* is drawn from Shakespeare's own sorrow at the death of his son Hamnet, though Shakespeare also wrote plays in which loved children die and are lamented before he lost his own son, such as *3 Henry VI* and *Richard III*.[81] Finally, there is the concept (expressed in the first *Attempt*) that *Twelfth Night* is Shakespeare's last play, 'composed at leisure' when Shakespeare was in retirement in Stratford-upon-Avon, as illustrated by the fact that its characters 'are finished to a higher degree of dramatick perfection' than those in any of the other comedies.[82] The idea of *Twelfth Night* as a retirement play was silently dropped in the last *Attempt* when Malone redated the play to 1607. Gordon McMullan draws attention to the way that Malone came to read the sequence of Shakespeare's plays that he had created as the narrative of its author's personal history.[83] It should be added that Malone read each *different* version of the sequence he came up with as the story of Shakespeare's life; he reinterpreted that story when he changed the sequence. Over time, Malone's sympathy for Shakespeare's supposed feelings was combined with his belief in Shakespeare's regular improvement: sometimes, rather than creating a sequence that could be read biographically, he may have used biography to create his ordering of sequence.

---

[81] *Attempt* (1778), 288. See also *Two Gentlemen of Verona*, described, in *Attempt* (1790), 298, as having 'that elegant and pastoral simplicity which might be expected from the early effusions of such a mind as Shakspeare's, when employed in describing the effects of love'; *Attempt* (1790), 312.

[82] *Attempt* (1778), 344.

[83] Gordon McMullan, *Shakespeare and the Idea of Late Writing* (Cambridge: Cambridge University Press, 2007), 129.

Even Malone's thoughtful explanations as to why so many Folio plays had not been printed in Shakespeare's lifetime relied on a preconceived sense of biography, in this instance combined with social history. He knew that Shakespeare had become a shareholder of the Globe playhouse in 1603, and that fewer of Shakespeare's plays had been published thereafter; he therefore determined that, after 1603, it was no longer in Shakespeare's interest to publish his plays, 'manuscript plays being then the great support of every theatre'.[84] That may indeed be the case (though why earlier publication would be in Shakespeare's or the company's interest needs to be asked): the King's Men appear to have owned 'their' plays and on occasion 'stayed' later publication, but the story of Shakespeare's earlier plays, whether owned and published by him or published by the company as part of advertising, remains frustratingly obscure. It is, though, intriguing to see how Malone's increasing knowledge of details of Shakespeare's biography became the explanation for the information he had to hand, so that, once again, the chronology was both suggesting biography and being moulded around it.

Another of Malone's biographical decisions was to assign plays for which he had no other strong information to a year that would otherwise be 'empty'. This informed his choice first of 1609 and then 1610 for *Cymbeline* – as 'I have found ... little internal evidence by which its date may be ascertained', and likewise 1609 (first *Attempt*) and 1610 (second and third *Attempt*) for both *Coriolanus* and *Timon* jointly because 'unless these pieces were then composed' Shakespeare would have 'been unemployed' at that time.[85] Behind this is the notion that Shakespeare wrote at an even pace throughout his adult life, producing roughly two plays a year with no gaps. As Leeds Barroll has pointed out, however, personal events in Shakespeare's life or the lives of those around him – including plagues, royal deaths and theatrical closures – may have changed the pace of Shakespeare's writing (though that is, of course, to 'correct' potential biography with alternative potential biography).[86] It should be realised,

[84] *Attempt* (1821), 294. [85] *Attempt* (1821), 452; *Attempt* (1821), 468.

[86] J. Leeds Barroll, *Politics, Plague and Shakespeare's Theatre* (London: Cornell University Press, 1991), 19–20.

however, that the regular spread of plays over the years of Shakespeare's life, found in most chronologies, reflect assumptions traceable to Malone's belief about Shakespeare's continuous inspiration.[87]

There was one entirely different form of internal dating that Malone used only sparingly and very broadly: what we would now call 'stylometry' or 'stylometrics' – the study of Shakespeare's rhetorical and stylistic habits, and what they can reveal about date order and sequencing. Malone was anxious to identify Shakespeare's stylistic tendencies but, in a pre-computer age, could only trace the broadest of habits over the dramas. He did, however, 'cluster' texts that displayed what he deemed to be similar verbal devices. His groupings also reflected dates that he had established for other reasons, of course. So, in the second *Attempt*, in which Malone had dated *Winter's Tale* to 1604, he noted that the text's metre was 'less easy and flowing' than many of the other dramas and that the phraseology was 'involved and parenthetical'; he felt that the text's general 'harshness' made it 'strongly resemble[e] *Troilus and Cressida*, and *King Henry the Eighth*, which I suppose to have been written not long before'.[88] Yet when he changed his mind about the date of the play because of new external information (Herbert's reference to Buc's allowing of the play, documented in Section 2), he also dropped that comparison: he found, instead, that the text resembled a different set of dramas, comparing its versification to that of *Cymbeline* and *The Tempest*.[89] It is at this moment, late in Malone's own life, that he creates the category of 'late style'; 'without Malone's painstaking work on chronology' as Gordon McMullan observes, 'there could be no late Shakespeare'.[90] But it is intriguing

---

[87] Taylor and Loughnane, 446, and Wiggins, *British Drama: A Catalogue*, 5: 59, both suggest, instead of continuous inspiration, a period in Shakespeare's writing between late 1601 and 1604, during which only one sole-authored play was produced: the former, *Troilus and Cressida* (though they also see him revising and adapting several plays over that time); the latter, *Measure for Measure*.

[88] *Attempt* (1790), 352.   [89] *Attempt* (1821), 453.

[90] McMullan, *Shakespeare and the Idea of Late Writing*, 136. Late Shakespeare is further questioned in Andrew J. Power and Rory Loughnane ed., *Late*

that Malone only became alert to 'late style' when he had a particular set of plays he had already deemed to be late, and that *Twelfth Night* was first part of, and then ceased to be part of, this group: a reminder that groups of texts can be found to connect stylistically with one another in telling ways when it has already been decided that they do so.

Another cluster Malone worked on, again having already determined a rough chronology, was 'our author's earliest productions'. *The Comedy of Errors*, *A Midsummer Night's Dream*, *Love's Labour's Lost*, *The Two Gentlemen of Verona* and *Romeo and Juliet* used 'alternate rhymes', which Malone thought not just early but modelled on the verse of what he believed to be Shakespeare's earliest texts: *Venus and Adonis* and *The Rape of Lucrece*.[91] He used his observations about rhyme to redate *Taming of the Shrew* from 1606, its position in the first *Attempt*, to 1594, because 'more experience of our author's style and manner' had persuaded him that *Taming of the Shrew* shared 'a frequent play of words' as well as 'a . . . doggrel measure' with *The Comedy of Errors*, *Love's Labour's Lost* and *The Two Gentlemen of Verona*.[92] But his pejorative emphasis on what he thinks 'doggerel' shows how personal was this judgement: to Malone, predictable rhyme was unpleasing, hence unsophisticated and a sign of youthful writing. His stylometry thus came to reinforce his sense of Shakespeare's literary development, in which the author 'rose from mediocrity to the summit of excellence; from artless and uninteresting dialogues, to . . . unparalleled compositions'.[93] That sense of the roughness of Shakespeare's early texts meant that Malone did not consider other reasons why texts might adopt punning and rhyme: genre, subject matter, particular actors, particular playhouses or audiences. He also did not consider that those texts might not be early at all. (*The Taming of the Shrew* is notoriously difficult to date.) When Malone frankly acknowledged that his verse observation 'must . . . be but a fallible criterion; for the *Three Parts of K. Henry VI.* which appear to have been among our author's earliest compositions, do not abound in rhymes', his solution

Shakespeare, 1608–1613 (Cambridge: Cambridge University Press, 2012), which demonstrates the late plays' diverse nature.

[91] *Attempt* (1790), 289. [92] *Attempt* (1790), 291. [93] *Attempt* (1778), 270–1.

was not that he was mistaken but that Shakespeare must have been the corrector, rather than the originator, of at least two of the *Henry VI* plays.[94] To 'periodise' Shakespeare's habits (and likewise to 'excuse' a play for not having those habits) is logical, though as a sign of the fallibility of Malone's rules, it must raise questions about the rules themselves.

Malone even used his fledgling stylometric analyses to embark on a very early version of attribution studies. On the basis of verbal parallels, in conjunction with Greene's rage at 'Shake-scene', he concluded of the *Henry VI* plays that 'Greene [was] the author of one of the elder [*Henry*] plays, and Marlowe of the other, or that celebrated writer [Marlowe] the author of them both': the first outing of the Marlowe attribution latterly revisited in Taylor and Loughnane's 'Canon and Chronology' study.[95] Another attribution Malone suggested concerns *Henry VIII*. Noting the text's large number of feminine endings, he followed Samuel Johnson in conjecturing that Ben Jonson had had a hand in the text, not least because the prologue to *Henry VIII* sneers at devices Shakespeare often readily employs, such as '*A noyse of Targets*', and a '*Fellow in a long Motley Coate*' (TLN 16–17): he viewed these comments as signs that Jonson was reviving the Shakespeare play but sneakily attacking its author in the process.[96] Given how conscious Malone was of Fletcher's echoing of Shakespeare, it is odd that he did not suspect that Fletcher was the co-author of *Henry VIII*, as is generally thought now; that is presumably because he had already decided that the play of *Henry VIII* originally had an earlier date.

That the words used, and the order in which they are arranged, are the strongest witness to when text were first written makes sense. But as these instances have collectively shown, Malone confronted enormous difficulties in even determining what constituted internal information: it may not actually

[94] *Attempt* (1778), 280–1.

[95] *Attempt* (1821), 315. Taylor and Loughnane, drawing on and developing upon work by Craig, Burrows, Nance and Segarra, et al., attribute *2 Henry VI*, *3 Henry VI*, and *1 Henry VI*, to Shakespeare, Marlowe and another unidentified hand, 493–499, 513–17.

[96] *Attempt* (1821), 400, 397.

be there (it may be being imposed rather than found); if there, it may not be datable; if there and datable, it may date a passage, rather than a text; and that passage may itself have been written before or after the rest of the drama. In his attempt to discover internal information, Malone sometimes forced links that were questionable and sometimes leapt to conclusions that he then, on consideration, retracted; he often used information to date one play that he rejected for dating another play. But Malone's very notion that Shakespeare wrote texts filled with topical allusions – a code only crackable by an expert long after their referent had been forgotten – is so open to question that S. Schoenbaum proposed that 'internal evidence can only support hypotheses or corroborate external evidence', rather than provide evidence in its own right; and Leeds Barroll argued for rejecting it as a dating category altogether.[97]

The trouble is that as Shakespeare did not write in a vacuum, his work must in some way reflect the moment of writing; yet the examples supplied here (there are many more of each kind) have illustrated how difficult it is to find secure, trustworthy information and how often, on further consideration, it proves to be slight and untrustworthy. All internal information requires a higher level of interpretation than external information, and as all interpretation is, in its nature, debatable, so almost all internal information is troubled, not least because a text's 'internal' dates often query rather than bolster the date supplied by external information. Nevertheless, topical allusion, and indeed many of the allusions first discovered or promulgated by Malone, continue to be tentatively invoked in current editions, as Section 6 suggests, for the same reason that Malone used them: because there is no other material available.

4 The Folio and Internal 'Late Dates'

A special kind of difficulty besets Malone's assessment of internal evidence in Shakespeare's First Folio of 1623. His hunt for 'early' references, an extension of his search for the moment of writing, made him ignore what

---

[97] S. Schoenbaum, *Internal Evidence and Elizabethan Dramatic Authorship* (London: Arnold, 1966), 150; Barroll, 238.

was more easily datable in the Folio: signs of late and often post-Shakespearean revision.

To start with, there is the fact that twenty-eight of the thirty-six texts in the Folio have been fully or partially divided into five acts, although texts published in quarto or octavo are in consecutive scenes.[98] The 'surprise' five-act structure of the Folio had long been observed. Samuel Johnson declared in 1765 that Shakespeare's plays 'were written, and at first printed in one unbroken continuity' and that in the Folio 'the common distribution of the plays into acts [. . . is] in almost all the plays void of authority' – by which he meant that the Folio's five-act structure did not sit comfortably on the texts themselves and did not appear to him to be 'Shakespearean' in origin.[99] Malone, who reprinted in his own *Works* Samuel Johnson's preface and the discussion above, was therefore conscious of the possibility that the texts that made up the Folio had been, apparently on a large scale, subdivided by non-Shakespearean hands. He does not seem to have addressed act structure himself, however, and when confronted with a sign of a new, Folio act break, like the one indicated in the Folio text of *Midsummer Night's Dream* by '*They sleepe all the Act*' (TLN 1507), simply avoided the issue: he opted for the quarto's stage direction instead, 'DEM. HEL &c. *sleep*'. He did, however, provide a footnote that he took, again, from Samuel Johnson, without adding further comment of his own, or rethinking the act division himself. Notes Johnson, as Malone quotes:

---

[98] James Hirsh in 'Act Divisions in the Shakespeare First Folio', *Papers of the Bibliographical Society of America*, 96 (2002), 219–256, details seventeen plays that are fully divided into acts and scenes, some imperfectly (*Tempest, Two Gentlemen, Merry Wives, Measure, Errors, Much Ado, As You Like It, Twelfth Night, Winter's Tale, 1 Henry IV, 2 Henry IV, Henry V, Henry VIII, Titus, Caesar, Macbeth, Othello* and *Merchant*); eleven divided into acts alone, two imperfectly (*LLL, Dream, All's Well, John, Richard II, 1 Henry VI, Richard III, Coriolanus, Shrew*). Seven are not divided (*2 Henry VI, 3 Henry VI, Troilus, Romeo, Timon, Antony, Hamlet*): his argument is that the process of division was not completed by the time the Folio was published, indicative of a semi-complete work of revision for readers.

[99] Samuel Johnson, *Preface* as quoted in Shakespeare, *Plays*, ed. Malone (1790), 1: 43.

> I see no reason why the fourth act should begin here, when
> there seems no interruption of the action. In the old quartos
> of 1600, there is no division of acts, which seems to have
> been afterwards arbitrarily made in the First Folio, and may
> therefore be altered at pleasure.[100]

These days the five-act division is thought Shakespeare's if in a play written for the Blackfriars playhouse, and is otherwise traced to one of two early modern adaptors: a prompter altering a Globe play to fit the needs of the indoor Blackfriars (which required regular act breaks so that the candles could be trimmed; Taylor), or a page adaptor – a scribe or perhaps an 'editor' in the printing house (who divided the text into acts to give the book a classical structure and appearance; Hirsh).[101] Either way, act breaks provide signs that Folio texts have collectively been (at least lightly) revised and manipulated after the time of first writing. Malone gave readers this information, but only in the voice of Johnson, and never considered its ramifications himself: that Folio texts presented a date range, not a date, and that that date range might extend right up to the time of publication itself.

On occasion, Folio texts (as with some quartos) preserved an actor name – rather than a character name – in stage directions and speech prefixes. Malone was delighted when the name aided him in dating a play early. Some names, however, helped date plays 'late': these he largely ignored.

So Malone saw that in the induction to the Folio's *Taming of the Shrew* there was a speech prefix for 'Sincklo'; he observed that 'Sinkler was an actor in the same company with Shakspere', and concluded that the surname had been 'inadvertently prefixed' here.[102] That inadvertency suited Malone, as John Sincklo's name is found in a Folio speech to *3 Henry VI*, and a quarto of *2 Henry IV* (1600): Sincklo was an actor of Shakespeare's time, and this internal evidence helped confirm Malone's dating of the

---

[100] Shakespeare, *Plays,* ed. Malone (1790), 2: 508–9; repeated in 1821.

[101] Gary Taylor, 'The Structure of Performance: Act-Intervals in the London Theatres, 1576-1642', in Gary Taylor and John Jowett, *Shakespeare Reshaped 1606–1623* (Oxford: Oxford University Press, 1993), 3–50 (17); Hirsh, 229.

[102] Shakespeare, *Plays,* ed. Malone (1790), 3: 249.

Folio-only text of *Taming of the Shrew* to the first half of Shakespeare's writing career. But in an important article on *Taming of the Shrew*, James J. Marino observes that though 'Sincklo' has, ever after, been used to confirm the play's early date, the line that he then speaks troubles attempts to date the play early. 'Sincklo', who performs the part of a strolling actor in *Taming of the Shew*, is praised for a role he has earlier performed, that of 'a Farmers eldest sonne [. . . who] woo'd the Gentlewoman'. 'Sincklo' then identifies which role that was: 'I thinke 'twas *Soto* that your honor meanes' (TLN 206–211). But Soto, a comic farmer's son who woos a gentlewoman, is a character in John Fletcher's *Women Pleased with Kindness*, a play first performed *c.* 1620 – a fact Malone seems to have known, as he (or Boswell) footnoted Theobald on the subject, 'I take our author here to be paying a compliment to Beaumont and Fletcher's Woman Pleased.'[103] Yet this Fletcher reference is very confusing for, as Marino states, it means that 'the actor whose presence is taken for an early provenance speaks evidence for a later one' and that *The Taming of the Shrew* gives itself, at one and the same time, a speaker who provides a Shakespearean terminal date and a dialogue that is post-Shakespearean.[104] Marino's influential article explores the way the 'early' indicator has been accepted, while the 'late' indicator has been explained away: sometimes as a reference to a lost early play that provided the source to Fletcher's known later play, and sometimes as a 'late' insertion into an otherwise integral 'earlier' text. Wishful thinking, he suggests, is shaping most of these arguments, and the result is to downplay the most obvious possibility: that 'the Lord's summary, printed in 1623, might be an accurate statement about *Women Pleased c.* 1623', and that therefore some other post-Shakespearean writer, perhaps Fletcher (who wrote exclusively for the King's Men after 1614, seemingly as some form of company play-wright), may have had a revising hand in the Folio text that we have.[105]

Other actor indicators that Malone observed were in *All's Well that Ends Well*. That text has two speech prefixes in the text for Lord 'E' and 'G'; it

---

[103] Shakespeare, *Plays*, ed. Boswell and Malone (1821), 5: 367.

[104] James J. Marino, 'The Anachronistic Shrews', *Shakespeare Quarterly*, 60 (2009), 25–46 (27).

[105] Marino, 43–4.

later refers to Captain 'E' and 'G'. These initials, Malone decided, 'denote the players who performed these characters'; he then looked at the list of actors prefixed to the Folio, found the names Samuel Gilberne and William Ecclestone, and suggested that they were the performers 'to whom these insignificant parts probably fell'.[106] His point has been broadly accepted, and William Ecclestone is generally agreed to have been 'E'; whether 'G' is Gilberne or Robert Gough, as E. K. Chambers suspected, remains undetermined.[107] In his *Historical Account* of the English stage, where Malone did what he could to collate facts about the 'names of the original actors … From the Folio, 1623', he took his research into the two actors a little further.[108] There he noted that Ecclestone's name 'occurs for the first time in Ben Johnson's *Alchemist*, 1610', and that Samuel Gilburne is 'unknown'.[109] He did not feed his findings back into his discussion of 'E' and 'G', however, perhaps because that would have involved considering a date of around 1610 for the relevant sections of *All's Well that Ends Well*: much later, then, than 1598, 1598 or 1606, the dates he bestowed upon the play in the three versions of the *Attempt*. Actually, we now know that Ecclestone only started performing for the King's Men in 1609–11, and was briefly a player for Lady Elizabeth's Men,

---

[106] Shakespeare, *Plays*, ed. Boswell and Malone (1821), 10: 437. NB: This chapter aims to identify when, outside the three *Attempts*, Malone *first* made certain observations, with the following provisos: Malone repeatedly updated his Shakespeare criticism, and he expressed his ideas in a variety of places – it is easy to miss earlier or later examples; Malone's remarks are sometimes fused with those of George Steevens (towards the start of his career) or James Boswell the Younger (posthumously) – on occasion, it is not clear who precisely is making a particular point.

[107] E. K. Chambers, *Shakespeare: A Study of Facts and Problems*, 2 vols (Oxford: Clarendon Press, 1930), I: 450. Rory Loughnane, 'Thomas Middleton in *All's Well That Ends Well*? Part 1', and Gary Taylor, '*All's Well That Ends Well*: Text, Date, and Adaptation', *The New Oxford Shakespeare: Authorship Companion*, accept the suggestion that the actors are Ecclestone and Gough, 279, 339, 342, but do not use that information for dating the play.

[108] Edmond Malone, *An Historical Account of the Rise and Progress of the English Stage* (Basil: J. J. Tourneisen, 1800), 135–184.

[109] Malone, *An Historical Account*, 275; 268; repeated in enlarged form in Shakespeare, *Plays*, ed. Boswell and Malone (1821), 3: 217; 211.

returning to the King's Men in around 1613; and that, depending on who 'G' may be (Gilberne was a 'late' apprentice in 1605; Gough performed 1590–1611; but William Gascoyne was a musician of the King's Men by 1624), these references might date those particular bits of the text to any time up to the production of the Folio.[110]

When there were actor names to be found in the texts that were not also in the 'Names of the Principall Actors in All These Playes' prefixed to the Folio, Malone was not happy at all. He tended to quote what other editors had said on the subject, without adding anything himself or therefore having to consider the date range they suggested. So in *Midsummer Night's Dream* in the Folio, the prologue to the internal play of *Pyramus and Thisby* has a stage direction for '*Pyramus, Thisby, Wall, Moonshine and Lion*' who are to enter preceded by '*Tawyer with a trumpet before them*' (TLN 1924–5). Malone, who retains the quarto stage direction in which there is no Tawyer, simply footnotes Steevens:

> In this place the Folio, 1623, exhibits the following promp-
> ter's direction – *Tawyer with a trumpet before them.*[111]

In fact, William Tawyer (or Toyer) is on a list of musicians who worked for the King's Men in 1624; he was buried at St Saviour's Church, Southwark, the next year, as 'Mr Heminges man' – in other words, he was the apprentice to one of the actors responsible for putting together the First Folio, John Heminges.[112] Tawyer's name, a sign that *A Midsummer Night's Dream* in the Folio is, at that point, a 1620s text, would not have done for Malone, who did not pursue the name or its ramifications.

---

[110] For dates of these actors, see Andrew Gurr, *The Shakespeare Company* (Cambridge: Cambridge University Press, 2004), 228.

[111] Shakespeare, *Plays*, ed. Malone (1790), 2: 527; repeated in 1821.

[112] On that same list are other trumpeters whose names feature in plays as bit parts – Samuel Underhill, who is found in *Barnavelt* (1619) and *Believe as You List* (1631), and George Rickner, who is in *The Honest Man's Fortune* (1625). See J. P. Cutts, 'New Findings with Regard to the 1624 Protection List', *Shakespeare Survey*, 19 (1967), 101–7. Discovered by J. O. Halliwell-Phillipps, *Outlines of the Life of Shakespeare*, 2 vols (London: Longmans, Green, and Co, 1887), 2: 260.

Finally, but most importantly, there is the Folio stage direction for an actor's actual name found in *Much Ado About Nothing*. That text has an entrance for '*Prince, Leonato, Claudio, and Iacke Wilson*' (TLN 868) – the last apparently the name of the actor who played Balthasar the singer. Malone knew about Jack Wilson and the questions that that name raised: Alexander Pope, whose Shakespeare preface Malone supplied in his 1790 and posthumous 1821 editions, had suggested the Folio was set from 'the prompter's book' because 'in some places [the actors'] very names are through carelessness set down instead of the Personae Dramatis' and footnoted this *Much Ado About Nothing* stage direction to make his point.[113] At the segment of *Much Ado About Nothing* in which the stage direction itself occurs, Malone, as before, quoted Steevens without comment: 'the First Folio, instead of Balthazar, only gives us *Jacke Wilson*, the name of the actor who represented him'; in his history of the stage he adds, 'we know that *John Wilson* played an insignificant part in *Much Ado About Nothing*'.[114] Again, Malone does not pursue the reference, and it is not entirely fair to expect him to have done so – though as actors are more datable than social history, the fact that he did not actively investigate them all may suggest the date ranges they were offering did not fit his model.

John/Jack Wilson (1595–1674), however, was an important figure in Shakespeare's company because he was not just a singer but a composer. In fact, Malone knew this too, relating a story about 'John Wilson, a cunning musician' who penned a comedy in the 1640s; he seems not to have realised, however, that he was referring to the same person as the one in the *Much Ado About Nothing* stage direction.[115] Actually, John (or Jack) Wilson had also been apprenticed to John Heminges, but in 1611; he became the main songwriter for the King's Men from 1615 onwards, and musical settings by him survive for songs in plays by Shakespeare, Beaumont and Fletcher,

---

[113] Reproduced in Shakespeare, *Plays*, ed. Malone (1790), 1: 93; and Shakespeare, *Plays*, ed. Boswell and Malone (1821), 1: 13.

[114] Shakespeare, *Plays*, ed. Boswell and Malone (1821), 7: 59. Edmond Malone, *An Historical Account*, 279.

[115] Malone, *An Historical Account*, 163.

Ford, Jonson, Heywood and Brome.[116] In *Much Ado About Nothing* terms, then, Wilson, who in the character of Balthasar sings '*Sigh no more Ladies*' (TLN 899), might be a boy actor with a good voice – meaning the Folio's text is just post-1611, when the young Wilson joined the company – or a senior actor who sings music he has freshly composed, meaning the Folio's text is from 1615 or later. Yet Malone, secure in his knowledge that *Much Ado About Nothing* had been printed in quarto in 1600, simply avoided amalgamating his John/Jack Wilson Folio references, which reveal that version of the text to be, in part at least, later in date.

The Wilson reference, seen through, could have alerted Malone to the fact that there is a strand of 'lateness' concerning musical references in Folio texts more generally, which may have the King's Men's two theatres at its heart. The company's Globe playhouse had not been a sophisticated musical space: plays written for it from before 1609 have no inter-act music (or, indeed, act breaks) and employ only the simplest onstage musical accompaniment, often limited to trumpets.[117] Indeed, when the play *The Malcontent* was moved from the musical Blackfriars and repurposed for the Globe in 1604, it had to have its musical interludes extracted; new dialogue was then added 'to abridge' as Richard Burbage – metatheatrically playing himself – explains, 'the not received custome of musicke in our Theater'.[118] When Shakespeare's own company had started performing in the Blackfriars in late 1608–9, it had, conversely, needed to ratchet up the music in all texts: partly because music was what the coterie Blackfriars audience, trained by boy performance, expected; and partly because music

---

[116] John Wilson was bound on 18 February 1611 to John Heminges and became free of the Grocers on 21 October 1621. See 'Apprentices', in Richard Dutton, *Shakespeare's Theatre: a History* (Hoboken, NJ: Wiley Blackwell, 2018), 32. For the range of composers he wrote for, see Keith Green, 'John Wilson's Music for Richard Brome's The Northern Lass', *Early Modern Literary Studies*, 20 (2018), 2; and Tiffany Stern, *Documents of Performance* (Oxford: Oxford University Press, 2009), 149–50.

[117] Richard Hosley, 'Was There a Music-Room in Shakespeare's Globe', *Shakespeare Survey*, 13 (1960), 113–23 (117–8).

[118] John Marston, *The Malcontent* [. . .] *With the Additions* [. . .] *by John Webster* (1604), A4r.

filled the candle-trimming gaps that the new theatre required.[119] Alterations that add songs and music to Shakespeare texts, then, are likely to reflect additions to texts made for the Blackfriars playhouse.

In *Measure for Measure*, the song '*Take, oh take those lips away*' (TLN 1770–75) is the first part of a two-stanza song to be found in Fletcher and Massinger's *The Bloody Brother* (also known as *Rollo, Duke of Normandy*), performed *c.* 1617. While in *Measure for Measure* one might assume that the song, about a faithless lover, is about a man (it feeds the melancholy of Mariana, an abandoned woman), *Rollo*, which contains the second stanza, makes abundantly clear that the forswearer (and thus the subject of the song) is in fact a woman whose breasts are on prominent display:

> *Take, Oh take those lips away*
> *that so swetly were forsworne,*
> *And those eyes, like breake of day,*
> *lights that doe misleade the Morne,*
> *But my kisses being* [sic: for 'bring'] *againe,*
> *Seales of love, though seal'd in vaine.*
>
> *Hide, Oh hide those hils of Snow,*
> *which thy frozen blossome* [sic: for 'bossom'] *beares,*
> *On whose tops the Pincks that grow*
> *are of those that April weares.*
> *But first set my poore heart free,*
> *bound in those Ioy* [sic: for 'Icy'?] *chaines by thee.*[120]

Malone, who knew of *The Bloody Brother* connection with '*Take, Oh take*' – Theobald had pointed it out in his 1733 edition – noted, weakly, 'I believe that both these stanzas were written by our author', quoting a passage of *Venus and Adonis* in which lips are described as 'seals', as proof that the first

[119] The King's Men had occupancy of the Blackfriars from 1608, but performance does not seem to have started until later. See Irwin Smith, *Shakespeare's Blackfriars Playhouse* (New York: New York University Press, 1964), 247.

[120] John Fletcher and Philip Massinger, *The Bloody Brother* (1639), H4v.

stanza was Shakespearean, even though, as he also pointed out, the observation was commonplace.[121] He did not, however, address the logical problems with his claim: according to his argument, Shakespeare will have written a two-stanza song while alive, employed only one of those stanzas in his lifetime and left the other stanza to work its way – somehow – after his death into a new play (though that second stanza also has the effect of changing the gender of its subject). In fact, as both stanzas are loosely derived from a popular Latin poem '*Ad Lydiam*', and as it is more logical to subtract a stanza in order to make the sex of the hero unclear than it is to add a stanza that changes the sex of the hero, this song is almost certain to have originated in its two-stanza form in *The Bloody Brother*. It would, then, have been adapted for use in *Measure*: dating that bit of *Measure* to around or post *The Bloody Brother* date, 1617.[122] The song enters the text courtesy of an adaptor, who might, given the date and the origin in Fletcher's *Rollo*, be Fletcher himself, but is equally likely to be the singer and company composer John/Jack Wilson, whose setting of this particular song still survives.[123]

Then there are the songs in *Macbeth*, another text that is Folio-only. Two witches' songs in that text are introduced by first lines but are not supplied in full: one stops at '*Come away, come away, &c*'. (TLN 1467) and one simply requests '*Blacke Spirits, &c*'. (TLN 1572) The words of the songs, however, exist in Middleton's manuscript play *The Witch* (*c*. 1613–16), a text both Malone and Steevens had examined.[124] Because of his obsession with earliness, however, Malone had at first agreed with Steevens that Middleton's play must have preceded *Macbeth* and that Shakespeare had adopted its already-extant songs

---

[121] Shakespeare, *Plays*, ed. Malone (1790), 2: 85.

[122] See Frederick William Sternfeld, *Music in Shakespearean Tragedy* (London: Routledge and Kegan Paul, 1962), 90; and John Jowett's analysis of surviving song texts and their text and music variants in Appendix IV of Gary Taylor and John Jowett, *Shakespeare Reshaped* (Oxford: Clarendon Press, 1993), 272–95.

[123] Published in John Playford, *Select Musicall Ayres, and Dialogues, For One and Two Voyces, to Sing to the Theorbo, Lute, or Basse Violl* (1652), 2. The case for adaptation, using this Fletcher song, by Middleton in 1621 is made in Taylor and Loughnane, 554–7.

[124] Thomas Middleton, *The Witch*, ed. L. Drees and Henry de Vocht (Louvain: Librairie Universitaire, 1945), 42, 62–3.

shortly thereafter.[125] By the third *Attempt*, however, he had rethought *The Witch* and was now dating it to around 1613. He did not, though, acknowledge what his change of date must mean: that the surviving text of *Macbeth* must, at least around its songs, be in post-1613 form.

The song additions to *Macbeth* are likely to have entered the text as an aspect of music-specific adaptation, for another evident alteration to the *Macbeth* text is also musical. While in the dialogue of *Macbeth* only three witch performers are necessary, the '*Witches Dance*' (TLN 1680) is preceded by a stage direction request for 'the other three Witches' (TLN 1566), who then say nothing (though they may help sing the '*Blacke Spirits*' song). Their purpose, however, seems to be to take part in the dance, as it directly mirrors the passage in Middleton's *The Witch* where six witches are required to '*Daunce ye witches Dance & Ex*[*i*]*t*'.[126] *Macbeth* seems, then, to have been revised to take on the songs *and dances* from *The Witch*: in other words, it has been musically revised. Two men, depending on dating, are likely to have been involved in these musical changes: John Wilson, as addressed, or his composing predecessor for the company – and the man who presumably trained him in songwriting – Robert Johnson (*c.* 1583–1633). The music that survives for *The Witch/Macbeth* might be by Johnson or Wilson (as Wilson adapted and imitated Johnson, which of the two is the original composer is not always evident).[127] Certainly someone musically competent, with access to all the compositions for *The Witch*, seems to have lifted the music wholesale from one text to another. If the adaptations are musical, though, a playwright does not need to have had a hand in their migration, and Malone's notion was that the songs were 'perhaps in the possession of the managers' of the theatre and entered *Macbeth* that way.[128]

---

[125] *Attempt* (1778), 326–8.

[126] Thomas Middleton, *The Witch*, ed. for Malone Society Reprints by W. W. Greg and F. P. Wilson (Oxford: Oxford University Press, 1948), 89.

[127] See John P. Cutts, 'The Original Music to Middleton's *The Witch*', *Shakespeare Quarterly*, 7 (1956), 203–9.

[128] *Attempt* (1790), 363–4. That the play was revised as a whole in 1616 and by a playwright, Thomas Middleton, is the argument put forward by Taylor and Loughnane, 564–8.

Further musical habits that Malone did not follow up on at all were the potential reuses of court masques in plays – though Malone did remark upon the increasing popularity of the masque form in the time of James I and Charles I.[129] He did not, however, observe how often the masques in Shakespeare plays are not germane to the fictions in which they sit and seem to echo masques got up for single court performances. *The Winter's Tale* apparently houses a version of the satyrs' dance from Jonson's *Masque of Oberon* (performed on 1 January 1611) as its '*Dance of twelve Satyres*', for which music survives by Robert Johnson; *Macbeth's* '*Witches dance*', rehoused from Middleton's *The Witch* as explained above, seems to have come originally from the antimasque of women 'in the habit of hags, or witches' of Jonson's 1609 *Masque of Queenes*, for which there is also music by Robert Johnson.[130] As for the masque of ladies as 'Amazons, with lutes in their hands' (TLN 455) – which is to be found in *Timon of Athens*, where it has little to do with the story, and requires the introduction of several boys dressed as ladies who are not otherwise needed – it is almost certainly a cut-down version of the *Masque of Amazons*, readied but ultimately not staged, in 1618, because in the event 'neither the Quene nor King did like or allow of yt'.[131] Dating Folio texts from their internal masques would give musical 'revision' dates unknown to Malone and to us, as we tend to date revision

---

[129] Malone, *An Historical Account*, 89–90.

[130] Tiffany Stern, *Documents*, 150–1; and 'A Ruinous Monastery: The Second Blackfriars as a Place of Nostalgia', in *Moving Shakespeare Indoors*, ed. Andrew Gurr and Farah Karim-Cooper (Cambridge: Cambridge University Press, 2014), 97–114 (113). For the witches' dance, its music, and its potential connection with *Masque of Queenes*, see Walls, *Music in the English Courtly Masque*, 136; Andrew J. Sabol, *Four Hundred Songs and Dances Form the Stuart Masque* (Providence, RI: Brown University Press, 1978), 568; and Mary Chan, *Music in the Theatre of Ben Jonson* (Oxford: Clarendon Press, 1980), 209n.

[131] Nan Cooke Carpenter, 'Shakespeare and Music: Unexplored Areas', in *Shakespeare and the Arts*, ed. Stephen Orgel and Sean Keilen (New York: Garland, 1999), 123–35 (133) joins Cutts and Lawrence in thinking this music relates to *Timon of Athens*; Andrew J. Sabol, *Songs and Dances for the Stuart Masque* (Providence, Rhode Island: Brown University Press, 1959), 168, disagrees, thinking this music is for William Davenant's *Salmacida Spolia*.

from textual rather than musical cross reference. But in ignoring masques while trying to make other songs 'Shakespearean', Malone neglected to see a consistency of lateness – traceable to musical revision, and probably reflective of the new Blackfriars playhouse – to be found across Folio texts. And because he did not pursue the Wilson/Johnson option and downplayed adaptation altogether, the fact that composers are potential, and most obvious, play adaptors has not entered the field at all.

Other, subtler musical changes to the Folio have only recently been identified. David Lindley draws attention to the use of cornetts in Folio texts: the entries and exits for Portia's first two suitors in *The Merchant of Venice* are, in Folio only, preceded by a flourish of cornetts; 'Flourish cornets' (TLN 237; 596) opens 1.2 and 2.1 of *All's Well that Ends Well* too. Cornettists seem to have come with the Blackfriars musical ensemble, and cornetts, Lindley suggests, are instruments specific to the Blackfriars playhouse.[132] His notion that versions of texts with 'cornett' directions have been updated after 1608 for the company's new theatre, together with the other musical adjustments above, suggests that the new theatre brought about 'musical' revision of playtexts: a form of revision that need not (and for timing reasons, sometimes could not) involve Shakespeare; but also need not involve any other playwright either.

Other lateness signs in the Folio are the passages, usually stage directions, that appear to have entered the texts with readers in mind, such as 'massed entrances'. Massed entrances pool at the start of a scene the names of all the characters who will enter during it; they are found in three Folio texts: *The Merry Wives of Windsor, Two Gentlemen of Verona* and *The Winter's Tale*. In *The Merry Wives of Windsor* in the Folio, there is a scene in which Falstaff enters alone; other characters then come to him throughout, as the quarto makes clear. The Folio's massed entrance at the top of that scene, however, is '*Enter Falstaffe, Mistris Page, Mistris Ford, Euans, Anne Page, Fairies, Page, Ford, Quickly, Slender, Fenton, Caius, Pistoll*' (TLN 2480–2). 'Massed entrances' give a text a classical appearance

[132] David Lindley, 'Music and Shakespearean Revision', *Archiv*, 249 (2012), 50–64 (53). He makes a similar point about *Titus* (not discussed in the text here, as Malone did not know of the quarto for that play).

on the page, much as the five-act structure does. Only long after Malone's death, however, did scholars become alert to the fact that the scribe who worked for the King's Men from 1618 onwards, Ralph Crane, sometimes favoured massed entrances when preparing a play for the page, a habit of layout that he apparently learned from Ben Jonson.[133] Malone, who did not specifically know of Crane's involvement with the King's Men, was hardly in a position to notice this habit – or was he? Crane's penchant for 'massed entry' has been gleaned, amongst other sources, from a surviving play manuscript for Middleton's *A Game at Chesse* (1624), written out for 'the worthily accomplished Master William Hammond' by Crane. That manuscript is now in the Bodleian Library, where its shelfmark, 'MS Malone 25', suggests it was once in Malone's possession, though the precise provenance and cataloguing history of this manuscript is a mystery, and N. W. Bawcutt thinks Malone may not have owned it.[134] If he did know the manuscript, Malone could have observed scribal massed entries of the 1620s and could then have linked them to a Folio habit of the same period; if he did not, he will still have had the Folio evidence to contend with. Either, however, would have obliged him to recognise secure 'late' signs in conflict with chronology: another hand in Shakespeare texts (that of Crane); another

---

[133] Ralph Crane's scribal habits, including massed entries, are discussed in T. H. Howard-Hill, *Ralph Crane and Some Shakespeare First Folio Comedies* (Charlottesville: University of Virginia Bibliographical Society, 1972), 21, 79; T. H. Howard-Hill, 'Shakespeare's Earliest Editor, Ralph Crane', *Shakespeare Survey*, 44 (1992), 113–30 (127); and Amy Bowles, 'Dressing the Text: Ralph Crane's Scribal Publication of Drama', *The Review of English Studies*, 67 (2016), 405–427 (414–15).

[134] When published by N. W. Bawcutt as *Malone Society: Collections, 15* (Manchester: Manchester University Press, 1994), it boasted, 'This is of special interest to Shakespeare scholars; the First Folio texts of several plays are thought to be based on transcripts prepared by Crane, and this particular version of Middleton's play shows the "massed entries" (the assembly of all the entries in a scene at the beginning of the scene) found in *The Two Gentlemen of Verona*, *The Merry Wives of Windsor*, and *The Winter's Tale.*' That this may not have been Malone's text is raised on p. 7.

variety of textual change (for the page); and an additional late moment of adaptation (the preparation of the Folio).

Malone did notice, however, that some stage directions in the Folio were not – and could not be – authorial (and therefore had to have been added by other hands later). He wrote about the stage direction in *Macbeth* that says that the ghost of Banquo is to come '*last, with a glass in his hand*' (TLN 1657–8), though, in the speech that immediately follows, the last king holds a glass, but it is the *first* king who is said to be Banquo.[135] His explanation was that the 'players' were responsible for errant stage directions of this kind. He seems, by players, to have meant John Heminges and Henry Condell, the actors who sign the dedications to the Folio and are often thought to have put the book together; but players are the people least likely to add in unplayable stage directions. It is somewhat more probable that Ralph Crane or another transcriber, in trying to make complicated text more comprehensible on the page, came up with these specious directions – which are, then, 'reader directions', rather than 'stage directions'.[136] What is odd here is that by noticing that the texts were being altered, and by tracing that fact to Heminges and Condell, Malone too was seeing that there were 'late' interventions in the Folio. He simply could not address what that implied given his desire to find only internal evidence that would date first writing. Instead, he used the inaccuracy of stage directions to give him leeway to 'regulate' those small passages of text.[137] That editors can alter, add and change stage directions has remained a given ever since: stage directions are always seen as more malleable than the rest of the text, partly because (though the fact is seldom articulated) they are so much less bound to be authorial than dialogue and so much more likely to be late additions to the play.[138]

[135] Shakespeare, *Plays,* ed. Malone (1790), 1: 58.

[136] 'Reader directions' are discussed in more detail in Tiffany Stern in 'Inventing Stage Directions; Demoting Dumb Shows', *Stage Directions and Shakespearean Theatre*, ed. Sarah Dustagheer and Gillian Woods for Arden Shakespeare (London: Bloomsbury 2017), 19–43.

[137] Shakespeare, *Plays,* ed. Malone (1790), 1: 58.

[138] See Tiffany Stern, 'Stage Directions', in *Book Parts*, ed. Dennis Duncan and Adam Smyth (Oxford: Oxford University Press, 2019), 179–89.

Malone also thought that other varieties of Folio textual intervention were 'editorial' without addressing how that complicated the earliness of the internal information for which he was hunting. For instance, he knew that *Othello* survived in two texts: one supplied by the quarto of 1622 and one, somewhat different, in the Folio. A major strand of difference is that there is blasphemy in the quarto text that is largely absent from the Folio. As the 1606 'Acte to restrain the Abuses of Players' banned blasphemy being spoken on the stage, current thinking is that the 'swearing' quarto contains a text written before the 1606 Act (though published much later); the 'non-swearing' Folio, a text revised afterwards.[139] Malone spots the prudery at work in the Folio, and knows about the 1606 Act, but does not see it through to a conclusion: instead, it simply annoys him. He supplies a note for the very first (quarto) word of *Othello*, 'Tush': 'Thus the quarto, 1622. In the Folio the word "tush" is omitted.' Over the process of editing the text, he notes the removal of swear words and oaths in ever more exasperated a fashion: 'I have more than once had occasion to remark that the quarto readings were sometimes changed by the editor of the Folio, from ignorance of our poet's phraseology or meaning.'[140] Finally, he loses patience altogether. The quarto text, which he prints, has Montano saying: 'Zounds, I bleed still, I am hurt to the death.' True to form, the Folio omits 'Zounds', a conflation of 'God's wounds' and hence a blasphemous exclamation; but it also adds an incorrect 'stage' direction. Notes Malone, 'The editor of the Folio, thinking it necessary to omit the first word in the line, absurdly supplied its place by adding at the end of the line, "*He dies*".'[141] (Montano, who is present in the play's final scene, does not die in the drama at all; hence Malone's irritation.) To Malone, both revisions are signs of the hand of the person he here calls, in the singular, the 'editor' – though he still

---

[139] Shakespeare, *The First Quarto of Othello*, ed. Scott McMillin (Cambridge: Cambridge University Press, 2001), 44–5; Barbara Mowat, 'Q2 *Othello* and the 1606 "Acte to restrain the Abuses of players"', in *Varianten – Variants – Variantes*, ed. Christa Jansohn and Bodo Planchta (Tübingen: Max Niemeyer, 2005), 91–106.

[140] Shakespeare, *Plays*, ed. Malone (1790), 9. 217, 236.

[141] Shakespeare, *Plays*, ed. Malone (1790), 9: 517.

seems to mean one of the actor-gatherers of the First Folio John Heminges or Henry Condell. These days we tend to conclude that the 'necessary' removal of the oaths is the work of an adaptor, and that the errant 'reader' directions, as explained, are perhaps again an indication of an overzealous Ralph Crane.[142] Here, however, we see a Malone very much of the opinion that editorial interference had shaped the Folio, but not therefore ready to see the Folio as containing, and perhaps being a collection of, revised texts.

There are, however, a series of observations that Malone made that did arise from recognising forms of Folio lateness – though he was happiest when he could trace that too to Shakespeare. He maintained, for instance, that there was visible authorial revision to be spotted between the quartos and Folio in the case of *Romeo and Juliet*, *Hamlet* and *The Merry Wives of Windsor*. For other plays, however, 'I have not … met with any evidence … that the several scenes which are found in the folio of 1623, and are not in the preceding quartos, were added by the second labour of the author'; instead, 'I suppose the omissions to have arisen from the imperfection of the [quarto/octavo] copies.'[143] But this argument, contradicted elsewhere in his chronology, maintains that the Folio was printed from manuscripts established and fixed many years before publication – which would make it textually unlike the quartos that he thought were printed from manuscripts dated near the time of publication. The idea that the Folio was simply a more perfect form of the quartos freed Shakespeare from most revision, adaptation and any form of co-authorship. This even though on occasion Malone did address revision, as discussed. He even, again contradictorily, entertained the possibility that other, later authors had indeed adapted discrete bits or passages from the plays. His notion that the prologue to *Henry VIII* was by Ben Jonson for a 'revival' text, addressed earlier, allowed for paratext – like a prologue or an epilogue – to be later than the text it heralded. He further touched upon 'late' paratext when he doubted Shakespeare's hand in the Folio-only prologue to *Troilus and*

---

[142] Discussed in Michael Neill, 'Appendix B: The Texts of the Play', in his edition of William Shakespeare, *The Oxford Shakespeare: Othello* (Oxford: Oxford University Press, 2006), 405–33.

[143] *Attempt* (1821), 365–6.

Cressida, though he did not expend much energy on the matter: he merely quoted Steevens ('I cannot regard this Prologue ... as the work of Shakespeare') and Ritson ('I conceive this prologue to have been ... interpolated by some *Kyd* or *Marlowe* of the time; who may have been paid for altering and amending one of Shakspeare's plays').[144] He did not, however, consider what, by extension, late paratexts in the Folio might indicate more broadly: that the book itself contained several texts in 'revival' rather than original form. Any such consideration would have been anathema, for it would once more have raised the question of when 'the play' was written, what 'the play' is and, further, who 'the play' is by.

Perhaps it was Malone's uncomfortableness with the Folio's 'late' framework that enabled him to accept without question the eighteenth-century habit of relegating the front matter from Shakespeare's Folio, a crucial aspect of that book's presentation, to deep within the edition. By so doing, he could hide the fact that the actual Folio presents itself not only as 'late' but also as post-author: it is a tomb for a man who is dead but whose work lives on. Ben Jonson's opening poem, facing a picture of Shakespeare, is about the 'Graver' (engraver, but also a play on 'grave') of the Folio's deceased author; his poem, 'To the memory of my beloved, The AUTHOR MR. WILLIAM SHAKESPEARE', calls Shakespeare 'a Moniment, without a tombe', arguing that he is 'alive still, while thy Booke doth live'; Hugh Holland bemoans that 'he gone is to the grave' but adds, 'The life yet of his lines shall never out'; 'I.M.' says that Shakespeare went 'to the Graves-Tyring-roome' until the Folio burst on the scene like an actor's 'Re-entrance', while Leonard Digges writes that when 'Time dissolves [Shakespeare's] *Stratford* Moniment, / Here we alive shall view thee still.'[145] Collectively, this framework maintains the Folio's content is 'living' – suggesting that it is still participating in the life of the theatre, of which change, often in the form of revision, was a crucial aspect – while its author has long enough departed for a statue to him to have been planned, crafted and fixed into place in Stratford-upon-Avon in the wall above his

---

[144] Shakespeare, *Plays*, ed. Malone (1790), 8: 223.

[145] William Shakespeare, *Mr William Shakespeares Comedies, Histories, & Tragedies* ['the first Folio'] (1623), A2v; A4r; A5r; A6r.

grave.[146] Malone sunk this front matter deep within his editions: in 1790 he placed the dedications by Heminges and Condell after Alexander Pope's 1725 preface and before Nicholas Rowe's 1711 *Life of Shakespeare* (so adding them to a history of prefaces to Shakespeare), and put the preliminary Folio verses in a section of 'Ancient and Modern Commendatory Verses on Shakspeare' (treating them, then, as poetic historical documents, rather than key elements of a particular book). By 1821 the Folio's preliminary matter had been distributed yet more widely: Heminges and Condell's dedications to the Folio were in the second volume, between the 'list of the early Editions of Shakspeare' and 'Modern Editions'; while the commendatory poems were in the first volume, between 'additional Anecdotes' and 'Essay of Phraseology and Metre'. The Folio's one-page list of 'names of the Principall Actors in all these Playes', providing the names of major actor sharers who performed in Shakespeare's plays, is not actually supplied in either of Malone's *Works*, despite Malone's profound interest in theatre history. Presumably he struggled with the achronological order as well as contents of this actor list, which names performers who post-date Shakespeare altogether – such as Joseph Taylor, who only joined the company in 1616, the year of Shakespeare's death – and therefore draws yet further attention to the Folio's lateness as a book. Malone's choice of preliminary matter for his editions instead consisted of a preface by him, followed by the major eighteenth-century prefaces that had preceded his: by Johnson, Steevens, Pope. In 1821, further eighteenth-century prefaces were added. He thus turned the emphasis away from the Folio's valedictory and

[146] Lena Cowen Orlin in *The Private Life of William Shakespeare* (Oxford: Oxford University Press, 2021), chapter 5, makes the fascinating suggestion that the monument itself may have been commissioned during Shakespeare's life and even part-constructed by sculptor Nicholas Johnson. But even were that the case, a gap of time would occur between burial and fitting a memorial into place. The royal tombs of Elizabeth I and Mary, Queen of Scots, for instance, were only completed four years after their respective deaths. See Andrea Clarke and Karen Limper-Herz, 'The Making of the Tombs', https://blogs.bl.uk/digitisedmanuscripts/2022/02/the-making-of-the-tombs.html [accessed 18 July 2022]

post-Shakespeare framing to a celebration of up-to-date eighteenth-century scholarship at the heart of which was . . . himself.

By downplaying the factually secure evidence from the Folio – named and datable performers, songs and music (the very bibliography and theatre history that he otherwise loved) – in favour of 'early' internal information, often arising from questionable topical allusion, Malone compromised the play sequence he established. That internal evidence yields a date range is a crucial aspect of chronology that has recently been espoused in major work by Taylor and Loughnane, and, separately, by Wiggins with Richardson; but that the date range of Folio texts is usually (always?) to beyond the death of Shakespeare is something still not considered fully in editions, as the next section will show. 'Late' revision means, at the very least, Shakespeare and/or his company reworking some bits of text, and may well suggest post-Shakespearean revision altogether, by playwright, composer and/or other adaptor. Recognising any such revision, and then deciding whether or not it is substantive enough to amount to a datable moment of adaptation, moreover, also muddles all attempts to solidify order and sequence of 'writing'.

5 Problems with Malone's Method and Question

As seen, one of the supposed advantages of internal information was that it could apparently provide initial ('*terminus a quo*') dates – dates of composition, then, as well as dates of later interventions. In supplying early dates, however, internal evidence is thus fundamentally different from external information, which always supplies end ('*terminus ad quem*') dates from when plays were fully in existence and in a state to be performed or published. What Malone never fully confronted is the fact that internal and external information are not only about different kinds of dates but also about measuring different things: the order in which Shakespeare *wrote* his works and the *dates of extant texts* are not the same. Malone was, from the start, fusing two different chronologies – work and text – into one, as though they presented equivalent information: they do not.

The trouble with merging these two different sets of information becomes instantly clear when we see external evidence – which shows when a work of that name existed – used to date a surviving text, even when that text internally suggests a different date range. Malone has been shown confronting that issue when receiving information late in life that obliged him to rethink conclusions he had drawn from internal evidence. So, his sense that *Othello* dated from 1611 and *The Tempest* from 1612 (*Attempt* 1 and 2) – information he based on internal references in the respective texts – was trumped when he learned that works with those names had been performed earlier, in 1604 and 1611, respectively. He assumed that the evidence he had found in the texts was no longer valid and he redated *Othello* and *The Tempest* accordingly, though by doing so he raised questions about all other dates based on internal evidence, of course. As the external evidence revealed a definite earlier moment of composition, and as Malone was asking when the plays were written, he could not do otherwise. But did the new dates, now treated as superior to Malone's internal examinations, sit comfortably on the actual texts he had examined? What Malone could not use this potentially conflicting evidence to highlight – as then his chronology would fall apart – was that external information was often not matched by internal information because the work referred to by the external information was not the version that had survived; which is to say that the texts that have come down to us, and that Malone had analysed, may indeed date from around 1611 and 1612, for the external evidence could refer to earlier, no-longer-extant versions of those plays.

The need for dates extracted from external information to outrank dates extracted from internal information is the direct result of problems caused by the question Malone was asking: when were the plays written? If external information yielded an earlier date for a play, he had to accept it, in spite of what the internal evidence had suggested.

Behind Malone's question about the date of each play were further challenging assumptions: the main one being that every play *has* an identifiable date (of first writing? of conclusion?) and is completed in a sequence before or after another datable play. But the very idea that a play has *a* date, rather than a range of dates, and a moment of completion, rather than – with revision and revival – several, is challenging. Even a poem said to have come into being on a known date, William Wordsworth's 'Lines Composed a Few Miles above Tintern Abbey, On Revisiting the Banks of the Wye during a Tour. July 13, 1798' is subject to hefty debate: when/where/if on the walk to/from Bristol could Wordsworth have written this – and is its date a record of the day when Wordsworth visited the Abbey or when he completed the 'lines', given that he elsewhere said that the poem had taken five days to come into being?[147] A play is, as a given, always created over a time-period. Even putting issues such as revision aside, if produced with no glitches at all, a play is likely to have been plotted first, introduced to the company in plot form, potentially revised in plot form; then written, which might take weeks, months or (Malone suggests with *Romeo and Juliet*) years; then read to the company, a process that might lead to further revision; then performed – with more alterations made in the light of audience response.[148] Already in this relatively uninflected depiction of writing a play, 'the date' of writing might cover a substantial period of time during which other plays may also join the sequence. Once we add in what the company was then likely to do – send the text to the Master of the Revels for approval and censorship, perhaps have the play rewritten in the light of that censorship, possibly then mark up the text for staging, certainly divide it into separately written actors' parts and attendant documents, all of which might in principle then be separately revised – we are far from 'a date' of writing. That, moreover, is only the start of a play's life if it performs successfully on the stage.

For there seem to have been several occasions on which a play might be revised, though, as shown, Malone was not keen to think about the matter. First, as Richard Dutton has argued compellingly, plays might be rewritten and elaborated for court performance: meaning that there will have been a different public theatre and court version of the plays.[149] Public theatre revival, when old plays are spruced up for popular performance, though not

---

[147] See Nicholas Halmi ed., *Wordsworth's Poetry and Prose* (New York: Norton, 2016), 65.

[148] Plot scenarios are described in Tiffany Stern, *Documents*, 8–35; the rest of the process, from readings onwards, is described in Simon Palfrey and Tiffany Stern, *Shakespeare in Parts* (Oxford: Oxford University Press, 2009), 57–60.

[149] Richard Dutton, *Shakespeare, Court Dramatist* (Oxford: Oxford University Press, 2016).

considered by Dutton, also seems to have been a moment for revision, meaning that there might also be a public theatre form and a later public theatre form of a single play. Prologues and epilogues sometimes tell the audience about the adaptation the play has undergone for theatre revival, which might involve new authors too: Richard Brome's *Covent Garden* has a prologue that entreats the audience to take the same survey 'as our Poet took ... Some ten years since', but notes that then 'it was grown with weeds. / Not set, as now it is, with Noble Seeds'; 'some ... condemn'd it for the length', says the revival prologue to Fletcher's *The False One*, 'That fault's reform'd'; the revival paratext to Fletcher's *Island Princess*, in the voice of the new author, suggests modestly that 'it should be known / What's good was *Fletchers*, and what ill his owne'.[150] Revival was another moment when substantial revision could take place; the adaptation regularly identified by Taylor and Loughnane in surviving texts may be for court performance or public theatre revival (the one might also become the other).

There was also the moment for revision in the light of the first performance, shaped to audience feedback, hinted at by Middleton, who advises the gallant in *Ant, and the Nightingale* to see 'the first cut of a Tragedie' (suggesting a second will follow); by Marston, whose *Antonio and Mellida* asks his original audience to 'polish' his scenes; by Jonson, whose *Every Man Out of His Humour* is given a new ending in his 1600 quarto because 'many seem'd not to rellish' the conclusion the play had had 'at the first Playing: ... and therefore 'twas since alter'd'.[151] The fact that so many prologues and

---

[150] Richard Brome, *Covent Garden* in *Five New Playes* (1659), A3v; Francis Beaumont and John Fletcher, *Comedies and Tragedies* (1647), 2P3v, 3M3v. Dutton's suggestion, *Shakespeare, Court Dramatist*, 154–5, 161, that Fletcher's *The Tamer Tamed*, when revived twenty-two years after first performance, will have employed the old text, and reused actors' parts kept from *c.* 1611 to 1633 is, given passage of time, changes in company personnel and habits of revising Fletcher's texts, unlikely.

[151] Thomas Middleton, *The Ant, and the Nightingale: or Father Hubburds Tales* (1604), D2v; John Marston, *Antonio and Mellida* (1602), B1v; Ben Jonson, *The Comicall Satyre of Every Man Out of His Humor* (1600), R3r. See Tiffany Stern, 'Prologues, Epilogues and Interim Performances' in *Documents*, 81–119.

epilogues are specifically for first performances seems to be to fend off, or, if necessary, shape the revision that may then occur. There might also, then, be a first performance and subsequent performance version of a play.

There seem, too, to have been occasions when casual, lesser revisions were made to plays. In 1983, John Kerrigan, looking at the kinds of changes found between Quarto and Folio *King Lear*, identified Shakespeare as a playwright who 'tinkered'.[152] That kind of non-occasion-specific fiddling is also suggested by accounts of the time. Nicholas Downie, in an encomium to the unperformed play *Sicily and Naples*, congratulates it for not being mounted in the playhouse where 'some *Players* braine ... Do's clap each terme new fancies on it's backe'.[153] His notion that actors' revisions are made in each of the three law court terms that governed a single playing season is probably an exaggeration, but revision to legal (and performance) 'terms' was a known habit: Ann Merricke writes excitedly to Mrs Lydall, in 21 January 1638, 'I could wish myself with you ... to see *The Alchemist*, which I hear this term is revised' (though this may, of course, be a reference to a full revival).[154] When Chamberlain in a letter to Sir Dudley Carleton notes that no new plays are pleasing audiences so that the 'Poets' are 'driven to furbish over theyre old', he confirms that revision to keep an old play going was a fairly normal event in the life of a popular play.[155] How and when revisions were recorded in the written text, as opposed to the performance, however, is a question: it may have taken a court performance or a formal revival for new words to be formally written down.

Whether a lightly rewritten play then needed fresh approval of the Master of the Revels is also open to question. Dutton maintains that any changes in the play as performed 'had to be reflected in the "allowed

---

[152] John Kerrigan, 'Revision, Adaptation, and the Fool in King Lear', in *The Division of the Kingdoms: Shakespeare's Two Versions of 'King Lear'*, ed. Gary Taylor, and Michael Warren (Oxford: Clarendon Press, 1983), 195–239.

[153] S. H., *Sicily and Naples* (1640), A1r.

[154] J. Munro, ed. *The Shakspere Allusion Book*, 2 vols (London: Chatto and Windus, 1909), 1: 443.

[155] John Chamberlain, *Letters*, ed. Norman E. McClure, 2 vols (Philadelphia: American Philosophical Society, 1939), 1: 567.

book"' – the version of the text signed with the Master of the Revels' imprimatur – and that even minor changes would occasion costly new approval, for which reason he thinks revision was rare and limited to special occasions.[156] N. W. Bawcutt, however, editor and (re)discoverer of surviving texts of Henry Herbert, Master of the Revels, draws a different conclusion: that the Master of the Revels returned texts to the playhouse asking 'the dramatist to make local revisions to cope with his instructions', and hence that texts were revised post-approval as a matter of course. He also does not think the Master of the Revels regularly called back manuscripts, concluding '[his] frequent warnings that the licence would not be valid if his instructions were disobeyed suggest that he did not ask for a second look at the manuscript'.[157] If substantial changes, like entire new scenes, were made, as for (some) revivals, clearly the Master of the Revels will have needed to approve the text anew, but an isolated account concerning a Shakespeare play is instructive. When the approved book of *The Winter's Tale* was lost in 1623, the Master of the Revels reallowed it, sight unseen, 'on Mr. Hemmings his worde that there was nothing profane added or reformed'.[158] In this instance, Herbert enquires into profanity, the kind of thing he might need to censor, but does not ask about other potential changes, and decides not to see the text. This suggest that, after submission to the Master of the Revels, and thereafter, there remained moments for textual fiddling. Which version of a text makes its way to quarto and Folio, and what relationship it has to moment of first writing – whatever that might mean – are, then, open to debate.

And, once one accepts, as Malone sometimes had to, that minor and major revisions happened to plays and that Shakespeare was himself one of the revisers, even greater problems emerge. Revision gives works a sliding date – a date when written, and further dates when written again; choosing which of those dates is the substantive one is further confused if

---

[156] Dutton, *Shakespeare, Court Dramatist*, 158.

[157] N. W. Bawcutt, ed., *The Control and Censorship of Caroline Drama: The Records of Sir Henry Herbert, Master of the Revels, 1623–73* (Oxford: Oxford University Press, 1996), 69.

[158] Quoted Bawcutt, ed., *The Control and Censorship*, 142.

Shakespeare is thought, himself, to be the adaptor. 'How', asks de Grazia, 'can we assign each play a single date when by some estimates Shakespeare revised after publication as many as sixteen of the plays ascribed to him?'[159] Indeed, in light of regular revision, what does the question as to when a play was 'written' mean: when a sheet of empty paper was first written upon; when a quire of full text was given to a theatre company; when a returned quire of text was scrawled over or written afresh; when that text was itself reworked?

To seek to know when a play was written, then, does not make sense of a jobbing early modern playwright, for what, asks Jeffrey Masten, might 'composition' even be thought to include: '(Re)writing? Copying? Staging? The addition of actors' gestures on stage . . . '?[160] Similar problems beset the question of when a play was 'finished': Paul Werstine's *Playhouse Manuscripts*, which shows seemingly 'incomplete' and 'unplayable' manuscripts used to guide stage performance, suggests the very notion of 'first written' and 'completed' may not hold for early modern texts.[161] Indeed, the idea of careful writing to logical completion reflects the categorising, organising and methodological concerns of an eighteenth-century archival scholar obsessed with order and in need of a sequence that would reflect or suggest biography. Malone dared not see that external information could never tell him about 'the' but only about 'a' date, and that internal information might reveal a date range at odds with external information altogether.

Then, finally, there is the problem of the evidence itself. Conscious of the fact that, because there were 'so few' materials for his study, he had to gather 'into one view' all sort of facts, allusions, possibilities and notions, Malone sternly reminded his reader that his dates should be understood as 'probabilities' only; in his final *Attempt* he made sure to keep material he now rejected – together with the reason for its earlier acceptance and

---

[159] Margreta de Grazia, *Four Shakespearean Period Pieces* (Chicago: University of Chicago Press, 2021), 103.

[160] Jeffrey Masten, *Textual Intercourse* (Cambridge: Cambridge University Press, 1997), 15.

[161] Paul Werstine, *Early Modern Playhouse Manuscripts and the Editing of Shakespeare* (Cambridge: Cambridge University Press, 2013).

current dismissal – in his explanation, by way of showing the reader how easy it was to fall for a false lead.[162] Thus in the third *Attempt*, in which he dated *Twelfth Night* to 1607, he gave as his reasons: that the text contained allusions to Dekker's *Westward Hoe* (performed 1604; printed 1607); that the text's sub-title suggested Marston's *What You Will* (1607); and that the 'dramatick perfection' of the characters was such that the writing could not be early. He also noted that he no longer thought 'undertaker' dated the text to 1614, as addressed; nor did he think the references to the Sophy dated the text to after 1611 when Sir Robert Shirley, ambassador from the Sophy, returned to London (he noted that a play about the Shirley brothers and their travels, *The Travels of Three English Brothers* of 1607, had introduced the topic of the Sophy to London earlier). Questions about the actual date of the surviving *Twelfth Night* will be covered in Section 6. Each separate piece of information, including the rejection, which itself with its reference to a 1607 play bolsters that earlier date, is entirely different in nature. But each separate piece of evidence can come to seem a proof of the others; indeed, reviewers were to praise the fact that Malone's work 'comprehends every kind of evidence', because they saw the profusion itself as an aspect of his argument.[163] Naturally, accumulation of different evidence must be used when there are few single sources; but accumulation can have the dangerous effect of making a possibility seem like a proof, and can make each individual piece of information seem more powerful than it is.

It remains the fact that Malone asked an unanswerable question, gathered contradictory evidence, accumulated it, and pooled external and internal information to create a single sequence. It is fascinating and extraordinary that his approach to both kinds of evidence, and his method of combining them into one sequence, have in so many respects remained ours.

6 Chronology Now

This Element has been on Malone and his choices, but it has, by extension, also been on current chronologies, as found in single-volume editions and

---

[162] *Attempt* (1778), 271–2; repeated in 1790 and 1821.

[163] Anon, 'Notes' (1783), 405.

complete works, and their choices too. Irrespective of the conclusions they reach, they all mirror Malone in method in that they assume and sometimes produce one chronological sequence made by putting together plays dated by external and internal information. Some have recourse to his specific examples: many, as argued, produce an order roughly similar to that of Malone in his third *Attempt*.

For a start, complete works are still asking Malone's version of the sequencing question, with a focus on when plays were – that vague word – 'written': the Norton *Complete Works* is concerned with dating 'the composition of the plays'; *The New Oxford Shakespeare* sets out to reveal 'what Shakespeare wrote' and 'when he wrote it'.[164] The *Norton* and *New Oxford Shakespeare* are also complete works in which plays are placed in what is called 'chronological order', as is also the *Complete Signet Classic Shakespeare* edited by Sylvan Barnet (1972) and the earlier *Oxford Shakespeare: The Complete Works*, edited by Stanley Wells, Gary Taylor *et al.*, of 1986 (revised 2005). All such editions, then, eschew the early modern 'Folio' play order, which groups plays by genre, in favour of an order Malone designed: the first complete works to be published in chronological order (history plays excepted, intriguingly: they were in historical order) was Malone's posthumous 1821 edition. All such complete works place surviving texts in one sequence to show when Shakespeare's most substantive contribution was made; all consequently place side by side texts dated by external and texts dated by internal information, though the texts themselves may have profoundly different natures and date ranges.

The reason for putting a complete works in chronological order is ultimately eighteenth century in nature. It supposedly reveals how Shakespeare's genius took root – or, as one of Malone's contemporaries wrote, it allows one to observe 'the progress of genius, from its dawn to its meridian splendour'.[165] Modern 'chronological' volumes, maintaining that Shakespeare's sequence supplies literal biography and the story of

---

[164] Stephen Greenblatt, 'General Introduction', *The Norton Shakespeare*, ed. Suzanne Gossett, Gordon McMullan et al. (3rd ed.; New York: Norton, 2016), 58. Taylor and Loughnane, 417.

[165] Anon, 'Notes' (1783), 405.

Shakespeare's brilliance, repeat this theme. David Bevington, whose complete works are in chronological order within genre, explains how the order shows that '[Shakespeare] constantly explored new themes, perfected genres and moved on to new ones, and saw ever more deeply into the human condition'.[166] Gary Taylor and Terri Bourus say, of *The New Oxford Shakespeare*, that chronology 'allows readers to trace the development of [Shakespeare's] writing over time' and 'offers a kind of biography of his creativity'.[167] For Stephen Greenblatt, whose Norton edition is also in chronological order, the result is to 'identify Shakespeare's personal trajectory, to chart his psychic and spiritual as well as professional progress' and to make 'the author . . . the beloved hero of his own, lived romance'.[168]

As current complete works continue to use Malone's conceptual frameworks, so they take on various of his assumptions and bump up against the problems he had. His notion that an external performance record is of first performance is sometimes taken as a given, though most such records are for plays mounted at court (or at the inns of court), and for special Christian celebrations such as Christmas, Candlemas or weddings; they are particularly unlikely to have constituted the first *ever* productions, as it was usual for a play to be 'rehearsed' – which is to say tested, improved and shaped – in front of the general public before being chosen for a special event.[169] Dutton's idea that some texts are printed in court form supports the notion of rewriting for special occasions; and if printed texts are in 'special' or 'ideal' court form, then they are likely to survive in a version that is after, or

---

[166] William Shakespeare, *The Complete Works*, ed. David Bevington (4th ed.; New York: Longman, 1997), 77–8.

[167] Gary Taylor and Terri Bourus, 'Chronological Choices', in *The New Oxford Shakespeare: The Complete Works* ed. Gary Taylor, John Jowett, Teri Bourus and Gabriel Egan (Oxford: Oxford University Press, 2016), 48.

[168] Greenblatt, 'General Introduction', *Norton Shakespeare*, 60.

[169] Cases for and against the first recorded performance of *Twelfth Night* (at the Inns of Court) as a record of its first performance are presented in James Schiffer, 'Taking the Long View: *Twelfth Night* Criticism and Performance', in *Twelfth Night: New Critical Essays*, ed. James Schiffer (London: Routledge, 2011), 6. For public performance as court rehearsal, see Tiffany Stern, *Rehearsal from Shakespeare to Sheridan* (Oxford: Oxford University Press, 2000), 43.

changed from, their moment of first writing; revival introduces the same issues. Another Malone assumption is the one he drew about the relationship between printing and performance: that there was usually a sizeable gap between first performance and first printing. While that seems to make commercial sense, it is not true of masques and is not obviously true of particular plays, such as *Much Ado About Nothing*, apparently performed and printed in one year, either. So the assumption voiced by Peter Blayney that plays were published 'usually about two years after they were first performed', while likely, may also be at root a Malone idea.[170]

In terms of internal information, we often echo Malone's thought processes and discoveries, even to the extent of taking on some of his more questionable 'proofs'. Single-volume editions of *Romeo and Juliet* generally at least discuss dating the text from *the* or *a* historic English earthquake (or pick another earthquake); some single-volume editions of *As You Like It* still suggest that the weeping Diana statue is a reference to the water-prilling breast fountain mentioned by Stow.[171] Malone's 'equivocation' is still regularly called upon to date *Macbeth*, perhaps rightly, though a simple corpus linguistics search, using EarlyPrint, reveals that 'equivocation' itself dates from *c.* 1380 and was used regularly in literature before and throughout Shakespeare's lifetime (and later: it was current in the time the songs joined the text too); 'undertaker', having been rejected by Malone himself, is, conversely, never used to date passages of *Twelfth Night*.[172] Various single-volume editions, dating *Hamlet*, accept Malone's

[170] Peter Blayney, 'The Publication of Playbooks', in *A New History of Early English Drama*, ed. John D. Cox and David Scott Kastan (New York: Columbia Press, 1997), 383–422 and Lukas Erne, *Shakespeare as Literary Dramatist* (Cambridge: Cambridge University Press, 2003), 100.

[171] The earthquake, and that it might be the one from Mottingham in Kent in 1585, and so date the play 1596, is discussed in William Shakespeare, *Romeo and Juliet*, ed. René Weis (London: Bloomsbury, 2012), 36; William Shakespeare, *As You Like It*, ed. Michael Hattaway (Cambridge: Cambridge University Press, 2000), 166, refers to the statue.

[172] Anupam Basu and Joseph Loewenstein, with Douglas Knox, John Ladd and Stephen Pentecost, 'EarlyPrint', https://ada.artsci.wustl.edu/corpus-frontend -1.2/eebotcp/search/ [accessed 17 July 2022].

notion of an *Ur-Hamlet* probably by Kyd.[173] This is not to say that any of those decisions is wrong: many are brilliant, and many may well be correct. But it is to temper praise for Malone for finding these examples with the caveat that they are all debatable, and that in following them, we subsume both the majesty and the problems that characterise all of Malone's choices.

We also follow Malone's *method* even when finding new examples. We still, for instance, call upon bits of social history to aid in dating texts – though, as seen when Malone tried to establish dates from coach-use and mulberry trees, social history can seldom be tied to a particular time-period; looked into deeply it can often unmake the point it supposedly bolsters. Taylor, for instance, takes Paroles' line in *All's Well that Ends Well*, 'the brooch & the tooth-pick ... were [i.e. wear] not now' (TLN 161–2), as evidence for Middleton's authorship of that bit of the text – the argument being that brooches and toothpicks became unpopular only after Shakespeare's death.[174] But, for a start, Shakespeare himself maintains they are unpopular in *Richard II*, in which Richard says that love to him 'Is a strange Brooch in this all-hating world' (TLN 2732) (glossed by Malone as 'as strange and uncommon as a *brooch* which is now no longer worn'; though this may of course be about one brooch rather than all brooches).[175] To define the later unpopularity of brooches post-Shakespeare, Taylor word searches *Literature Online* (*LION*) and finds comparisons with other plays of the period where brooches are also thought old-fashioned. A corpus linguistics search on a different database, *EarlyPrint Lab* (which reprocesses searchable texts from *Early English Books Online* and includes many more non-play texts) for 'brooches' and 'toothpicks',

---

[173] Discussed by Zachary Lesser in *'Hamlet' After Q1: An Uncanny History of the Shakespearean Text* (Philadelphia: University of Philadelphia Press, 2014), 176–8. For the alternative suggestion, that the first quarto is based upon an early draft version, see Terri Bourus, *Young Shakespeare's Young Hamlet* (New York: Palgrave, 2014).

[174] Gary Taylor, '*All's Well that Ends Well*: Text, Date, and Adaptation', *The New Oxford Shakespeare: The Authorship Companion*, 343–4.

[175] Shakespeare, *Plays*, ed. Boswell and Malone (1821), 16: 165.

however, suggests the opposite. Brooches are prized in William Browne's *The shepheards pipe* (1614), where the loss and recovery of a magical brooch, amongst other things, is the subject of an eclogue; and in Thomas Cooper's *The vvonderfull mysterie* (1622), where the Reprobate wears sin gorgeously, 'as a *Brooch* in his fore-head or as a *Crowne* vpon his head'.[176] Toothpicks are, likewise, extolled in Gervase Markham's play *Herod and Antipater* (published in 1622, but performed between 1619 and then), in which Tryphon addresses a 'deare Tooth-pick' and wishes 'I had beene made of your condition' because the lovely Salumith picks her teeth with one.[177] These examples are themselves variously interpretable, of course – love/hate of brooches and toothpicks may be being used ironically in some of these texts (including Shakespeare's)? – but they illustrate how tricky it is to date social history at all, let alone use it to define moments in texts. Change databases once more to look at images rather than text, and it will be found that pictures of King James I, throughout the period, and probably in light of a popular portrait by John de Critz, regularly show him with huge brooches in his hat. So alternative databases allow reverse conclusions to be reached about social history. That is not to argue the rights and the wrongs of it either way but simply to say, first, that social history remains tricky for dating purposes, and, second, that method of research – choice of database and question asked of it – effects the answers found.[178]

Thus, just as Malone's conclusions were determined by the texts he had read, so conclusions traced to databases are determined by which databases are selected, what content they contain and how they are then used. True, one further method used together with any single database is accumulation, so that various approaches are brought together to make each chronological point: reject one, and the others may still stand. But accumulation was, of course, problematic to Malone himself (it is, too, how attribution and conspiracy theorists shore up their arguments). Accumulation is crucial

---

[176] William Browne, *The Shepheards Pipe* (1614), first eclogue; Thomas Cooper, *The Wonderfull Mysterie* (1622), Z4v.

[177] Gervase Markham, *The True Tragedy of Herod and Antipater* (1622), G2r.

[178] Basu et al., 'EarlyPrint', [accessed 17 July 2022].

but is as strong as the individual points so gathered and can have the effect of making an argument seem more supported than it is.

Here it should be borne in mind too how limited all databases of necessity are, and therefore how limited the questions that can be asked of them. Most manuscripts of the period are lost entirely; of those that survive, many have not been transcribed and are not, therefore, searchable; those that survive and are transcribed are not usually on the same searchable databases as print texts. But it is also sometimes forgotten that over 60 per cent the known *printed* texts of the period are not searchable either. Quite apart from the print texts absent from *Early English Books Online* (*EEBO*) are the texts that are there in facsimile only, and not transcribed: the *Text Creation Partnership* (*TCP*, a brilliant resource which has revolutionised current research by transcribing texts on *EEBO*) does not have the money to transliterate every work on its site, and some first, and most second and subsequent editions of books, as well as serials, foreign-language texts and others have not been rendered into modern typeface and cannot therefore be searched.[179] Add to this fact the number of texts that were published that are lost, and it becomes clear how contingent even conclusions based on the fullest of databases must be.[180]

In different ways, too, the troubles that Malone had with his primitive stylometric analyses are also found today. He has been shown confirming the sequence of the plays he had determined upon with stylometric proofs; when he reconsiders and changes the order of the plays, however, he has then been shown finding alternative stylometric proofs that confirm his new sequence. The same still happens. For instance, in Gary Taylor's 1987 'Canon and Chronology', *All's Well that Ends Well* is dated to 1604–5, his conclusions partly backed up using stylometrics; in the updated 2005

---

[179] Text Creation Partnership, 'About EEBO-TCP', https://textcreationpartnership .org/tcp-texts/eebo-tcp-early-english-books-online/ [accessed 17 July 2022]. See Ian Gadd, 'The Use and Misuse of *Early English Books Online*', *Literature Compass*, 6 (2009), 680–92.

[180] David McInnis suggests that between 1567 and 1642, at least 744 plays are known to be lost (and 543 survive), *Shakespeare and Lost Plays* (Cambridge: Cambridge University Press, 2021), 1.

edition, it is changed to 1606–7 partly for stylometric reasons; and in *The New Oxford Shakespeare*, bolstered by a new theory about the text's transmission, stylometrics are used by Taylor and Loughnane to date it to a 'best guess' of 1605 (date range of 1603-early 1606), and a second best guess, a date of adaptation of early 1622 (date range of 1616-middle 1622).[181] Taylor (latterly with Loughnane) rethinks the evidence that he once put forward three times, just as Malone did, and for the same good reason: that advances in his thinking and research over time has made him reorder his sense of chronology. But the rethinking, like Malone's rethinking, is also a useful reminder that information – even seeming evidence – remains open to (re)interpretation. Computer data and computer analyses seldom offer certainties because computer data, like any data, can be analysed in more than one way: it itself needs 'interpretation'. It is intriguing how often the different scholars quoted in *The New Oxford Shakespeare*'s 'Canon and Chronology' study come to differing results. Moreover, as de Grazia notes of all stylometric analyses, 'the results cannot be used to date the composition of a play, only to support or reject a prior chronological placement': for the fact of the placement too is dependent on the placement of the surrounding text, and shaped *by* as well as *to* the order determined.[182]

Many complete works still effectively string Shakespeare's plays along a continuum – broadly suggesting continuous inspiration – and still get into the hazy area where biography is used to explain, but may somewhat determine, some of the dates. Bevington, for instance, maintained that Shakespeare's 'earliest work' – not easy to define – shows an 'extraordinary ability to transcend the models from which he learned': the observation helps confirm the grouping.[183] This need not be incorrect, in that Shakespeare will have written in *an* order, and will have learned and progressed as he did so; but the certainty here becomes proof of the chronology, even with plays for which there is very little dating information, such as the Folio-only text of *The Comedy of Errors*. Likewise for

---

[181] Discussed in Gary Taylor, '*All's Well*', 340; and Taylor and Loughnane, 557.

[182] de Grazia, *Four Shakespearean*, 66.

[183] Shakespeare, *Complete Works*, ed. Bevington, 41.

Greenblatt, the plays written between 1600 and 1608, of which he names *Hamlet, Othello, King Lear, Macbeth, Antony and Cleopatra* and *Coriolanus,* show 'a major shift in sensibility, an existential and metaphysical darkening'; he suggests Shakespeare may have 'drawn upon a deep personal anguish, perhaps caused by the decline and death of [his] father, John, in 1601'.[184] This draws upon several texts – *Macbeth, Antony and Cleopatra* and *Coriolanus* – that are Folio-only, hence hard to pinpoint in date terms. Single volumes, too, can shore up their dates with biography: as when *Romeo and Juliet* is described as a dirge written by a bereaved Shakespeare in the light of his son Hamnet's death.[185]

Because of inheriting Malone's intense interest in 'earliness', we have been slow in other ways to notice the lateness of Folio texts in their entirety, forgetting that if Shakespeare's company continued to perform his plays over time, the texts are likely to bear witness both to Shakespearean and to post-Shakespearean adaptation. So, it is worth supplying again a full list of the eighteen Shakespeare plays that are Folio-only: *All's Well that Ends Well, Antony and Cleopatra, As You Like It, The Comedy of Errors, Coriolanus, Cymbeline, 1 Henry VI, Henry VIII, Julius Caesar, King John, Macbeth, Measure for Measure, The Taming of the Shrew, The Tempest, Timon of Athens, Twelfth Night, The Two Gentlemen of Verona* and *The Winter's Tale.* Dating any of these plays is tricky; dating the particular texts of them preserved in the Folio to any time before 1623 involves substantial reliance on internal information, with all the issues of interpretation that that suggests.

There have of late, however, been serious advances that have queried Malone's approach – or, rather, lack of one – to lateness and revision. Wiggins, in his landmark chronological survey of all early modern plays and entertainments, and Taylor and Loughnane, in their book-length rethinking of the chronology of Shakespeare's works in the light of questions about authorship and adaptation, both offer date *ranges* for some of the works they discuss, including date ranges for some 'additions', 'revisions' or 'adaptations' when identified. That welcome instability of range is, in both sets of work, shown to extend beyond Shakespeare's lifetime: a significant advance

[184] Greenblatt, 'General Introduction', *Norton Shakespeare*, 60.

[185] Shakespeare, *Romeo and Juliet*, ed. Weis, 36–7.

in the treatment of chronology. Taylor and Loughnane focus their interest in lateness on plays they also trace to adaptation by Middleton, however, and so look only at certain texts and with very directed findings in mind. Their important discussion of second, later dates for plays they argue are substantively revised/adapted raises questions about how to define 'substantive' – *Othello*, though it survives in different textual states, for instance, is not judged to merit a second date – and problematises the very notion of reading texts in the order in which they were composed rather than the different order in which they survive. And both Wiggins and the *New Oxford* editors also counter their date ranges with a narrow 'best guess' date for original composition, of necessity early, and often with a precision which opposes their thoughtful explications of textual fluidity elsewhere. For Taylor and Loughnane, their 'best guess' sometimes even suggests a specific period within a single year in which the play was written – early, late or in the middle – compressing what they elsewhere see as malleable texts to the briefest and most confined of writing periods.

Our inherited interest in earliness has also led us to ignore some of the information that suggests that plays known to have been written for the Globe may well have been overhauled for the Blackfriars playhouse. Certainly, though, there is a telling amount of documentary evidence that reveals how, long before the Interregnum, plays originally penned for the Globe had come to be seen as Blackfriars texts. Henry Herbert, Master of the Revels, received a 'benefitt' for a 'winters day' performance of *Othello* on 22 November 1629 – almost certainly, then, for performance at the enclosed Blackfriars, the open-air Globe being used for summer performances;[186] John Greene, in a 1635 diary, records going to Blackfriars playhouse to see 'Ffalstafe' (probably *1 Henry IV* or *2 Henry IV*; perhaps *The Merry Wives of Windsor*).[187] By the time Leonard Digges writes a poem about Shakespeare's performances of the 1630s, he says that other playwrights 'suffer' at 'Blacke-Friers' when compared to the wonderful staples there: 'when Cesar would appear' (*Julius Caesar*), 'Honest *Iago*,

---

[186] Bawcutt, *The Control and Censorship*, 169.

[187] E. M. Symonds, 'The Diary of John Greene (1634–57)', *English Historical Review*, 43 (1928), 385–94 (386).

or the jealous Moore' (*Othello*), '*Falstaffe ... Hall* [*i.e.* Hal], *Poines*' (*1 Henry IV* and/or *2 Henry IV*), '*Beatrice* / And *Benedick*' (*Much Ado About Nothing*) and '*Malvoglio* that crosse-garter'd Gull' (*Twelfth Night*).[188] These references, all to plays that we might designate 'Globe' texts, just shortly post-Folio, raise questions about which versions of the texts – for which playhouse – the Folio itself contains. Do its texts survive in the form in which they were performed for Blackfriars, and, if so, what might that mean? Have Globe plays simply been lightly tapped into shape in terms of stage directions and perhaps music, or might they have been more substantially changed – or something between the two?

It is worth adding that from the Restoration onwards most Shakespeare plays were thought of as essentially Blackfriars texts. James Wright, whose *Historia Histrionica* of 1699 recalls the great actors of the pre-Interregnum days, titles the players John Lowin, Joseph Taylor and Eliard Swanston, the 'Old Black-friers Men', and lists their key plays as *Falstaff* (again *1 Henry IV* or *2 Henry IV* – or just possibly *The Merry Wives of Windsor*), *Hamlet* and *Othello*.[189] And when Shakespeare's plays were parcelled out for renewed performance post-Restoration, it was with specific links to what was thought of as their prior place of performance. So the 1660 record of plays to be allotted to William Davenant's The Duke's Men calls them 'ancient Plays that were playd at Blackfriers': it names *The Tempest, Measure for Measure, Much Ado About Nothing, Romeo and Juliet, Twelfth Night, Henry VIII, King Lear, Macbeth* and *Hamlet*.[190] A matching document of 1668 detailing which 'part of His Ma[jes]tes Servants Playes as they were acted at the Blackfryers' should be 'now allowed of' by Thomas Killigrew's company, the King's Men, adds *The Winter's Tale, King John, Richard II, The Two Gentlemen of Verona, The Merry Wives of Windsor, The Comedy of Errors, Love's Labour's Lost, A Midsummer Night's Dream, The Merchant of Venice, As You Like It, The Taming of the*

---

[188] Leonard Digges, 'Upon Master William Shakespeare, the *Deceased Author, and His* Poems', in *Poems*, ed. William Shakespeare (1640), 3r–4r. Leonard Digges died in 1635, giving a terminal date, then, for the poem.

[189] James Wright, *Historia Histrionica* (1699), 4.

[190] Reproduced Smith, *Shakespeare's Blackfriars Playhouse*, 502.

Shrew, All's Well that Ends Well, 2 Henry IV, Richard III, Coriolanus, Titus Andronicus, Julius Caesar, Othello, Antony and Cleopatra and *Cymbeline*.[191] These, of course, are partial performance accounts, and the fact that Blackfriars had been an oblong, indoor, private theatre – bearing closer comparison to Restoration stages than had the round Globe – may explain why it was seen as the 'source' of the plays it hosted. Yet if, as these accounts insistently suggest, the main or important locus of performance came to be Blackfriars, it is worth asking when that became the case and whether all texts after around 1609–10, when Blackfriars came to be used for King's Men performances, were rejigged for the more sophisticated theatre – and, if so, in what way or ways. (Does 'Blackfriars' in these accounts refer to a repertory, or to a state of text, and is trying to draw such a distinction itself problematic?) This is a historical issue that Malone, a historian in approach, could have addressed in his chronology or his theatre history: he did not, but it is equally strange that it has not been wholly addressed since.

Instead, we have inherited certain ways of downplaying the 'late' information the Folio collectively reveals. Like Malone, we start our Shakespeare complete works with the modern voice and up-to-date opinions of the editor or editors; Folio front matter is seldom very near the front and is sometimes, as in *The Arden Shakespeare Complete Works* ed. Richard Proudfoot, David Scott Kastan, Anne Thompson and Henry Woudhuysen (London: Bloomsbury, 2021), cut out altogether.

Adaptation, an obvious 'lateness' sign, is something many chronologers are interested in, however, and that is in spite of rather than because of Malone – though we are still seemingly shaped by his choices. Malone was worried by the very notion of adaptation and did his best to avoid it and its implications. Haunted by the links he repeatedly found between the works of John Fletcher and Shakespeare, he comforted himself with George Steevens' odd notion that Shakespeare and Fletcher had never worked together, despite the fact that they are both named as co-authors on the title page of *Two Noble Kinsmen* (1634).[192] Whenever he found yet another Fletcher–Shakespeare parallel, he put it down to the fact that Fletcher was

---

[191] Smith, *Shakespeare's Blackfriars Playhouse*, 503. [192] *Attempt* (1821), 474–5.

a copycat who 'wrote in silent *imitation* of our author's manner'.[193] So he agreed with Steevens that Fletcher parodied Falstaff's death in his play *The Captain*; ridiculed Hamlet's soliloquy and Ophelia's death in *The Scornful Lady*; 'copied' a quarrelling scene from *Julius Caesar* in *The Maid's Tragedy;* referred to *Julius Caesar* in the prologue to *The False One*; and imitated a speech of Iachimo's from *Cymbeline* in *Philaster*.[194] But though these instances show Fletcher's internalisation of Shakespeare's linguistic and plot habits, he never therefore concluded Fletcher was a Shakespeare adaptor.[195] And, just as Malone avoided the issue, we have come up with our own rules about what to look for and how. In terms of adaptation, the case for Fletcher is still less comprehensively made than that for Middleton, perhaps because Middleton's work has been more recently edited than Fletcher, though Middleton's works do not show the same quantity or variety of overt Shakespearean links.[196]

That a main source of adaptation was along musical lines was not a Malonian thought, and, partly for that reason, seems never to have been fully realised later. John Wilson and Robert Johnson, the composers, are never considered as adaptors – yet plays in revival often contained new or changed songs, music, and related context.[197] What remains to be said is that when adaptation is thought about these days, the credit is always given to a playwright, not a composer – and nearly always a famous, known one at that.[198] But if

---

[193] Shakespeare, *Plays*, ed. Boswell and Malone (1821), 20: 239.

[194] *Attempt* (1821), 398, 449–50, 452.

[195] Declared on the titlepage of *The two noble kinsmen presented at the Blackfriers by the Kings Maiesties servants, with great applause* which is said to have been 'written by the memorable worthies of their time; Mr. Iohn Fletcher, and Mr. William Shakspere. Gent' (1634).

[196] It is worth noting that the editor who has most strongly promulgated the idea of Middleton as Shakespeare's main adaptor, Gary Taylor, is also general editor of *Thomas Middleton: The Collected Works* (Oxford: Oxford University Press, 2010).

[197] Tiffany Stern, 'Songs and Masques' in *Documents*, 120–73.

[198] Credit goes here to *The New Oxford Shakespeare*, that, as addressed, does attribute the three parts of *Henry VI* to some combination of Shakespeare, Marlowe and 'an other'.

'which playwright?' (rather than 'which composer?') is not the right question, or not the only question, then the answer it produces cannot be right: for the answers reflect the questions we have asked.

The great problem that troubled Malone's sequence and analysis – combining internal and external information – remains what happens with respect to some plays. That has redounded oddly against Malone of all people: we often feel as though we 'know' the dates of Shakespeare plays, and critics declare whether Malone, particularly in his first *Attempt*, is right or wrong using 'our' sense of chronology. For instance, we have fallen into the trap that Malone did in his third *Attempt*: we have found new external information that we use to redate not only when Shakespeare wrote that play (which is reasonable) but also the text that survives (which is not so reasonable).

An example is what we have done with the most notable 'hard' external information that we have acquired post-Malone: that for *Twelfth Night*. Malone's sense, from examining *Twelfth Night*, had been that the text he was reading dated from 1614 (first and second *Attempt*) or 1607 (third *Attempt*); he felt it bore 'evident marks of having been composed at leisure', and in the first two *Attempts* thought it Shakespeare's most perfect and hence last play.[199] All that changed when, in 1831, John Payne Collier published extracts from a barrister's diary he had found – we have since discovered the writer to be John Manningham – of 2 February 1601–2. Collier quotes Manningham as writing:

> At our feast we had a play called Twelve night or what you
> will . . .. A good practise in it to make the steward believe his
> lady widdowe was in love with him, by counterfayting
> a letter, as from his lady, . . . prescribing his gestures,
> inscribing his apparaile, &c. and then when he came to
> practise, making him believe they tooke him to be mad.[200]

---

[199] *Attempt* (1790), 383.

[200] As quoted in J. Payne Collier, *The History of English Dramatic Poetry to the Time of Shakespeare and the Annals of the Stage to the Restoration*, 3 vols (London: John Murray, 1831), 1: 328.

This record establishes the fact that a version of *Twelfth Night* was in existence by February 1601–2; and this is confirmed, say Taylor and Loughnane, through modern stylometric analyses; they provide no later revision date for the play.[201] Indeed, we have, since this discovery, ignored – even scoffed at – the evidence that Malone had used to date the text later. And, oddly, this is not a text typically considered as having 'late' signs, presumably because it is not clearly adapted by another playwright. But when does the surviving text date from, and how does it relate to that external date of 1601–2?

Twelfth Night is Shakespeare's most musical play. It begins with tune (the Duke's 'play on' [TLN 5] confirms that music is already playing); it ends with tune (the song 'When that I was and a little tine boy' [TLN 2560]); internally, it contains another two whole songs, 'O Mistris mine' (TLN 739), and 'Come away, come away death' (TLN 941), and a third, the catch 'Hold thy peace, thou Knave' (TLN 764); parts of other songs are sung throughout, and the tune to 'Come away' is also played as background music through most of the scene in which it features. As the Globe playhouse, in which Shakespeare's company was performing in 1602, however, was not a musical space – as explained in Section 4 – dating the surviving *Twelfth Night* to 1602 is tricky. The argument that the text is preserved in a special form, for the Inn of Court production Manningham saw or some other court production, does not easily work for this version of the text either, because it has evident signs of revision and hence of being later than its original moment of writing. Viola, washed up on the shores of Illyria, first introduces herself as a singer – 'I can sing' (TLN 109–10), she explains – but in the text that follows, she never sings; when Orsino asks her to perform 'That old and Anticke song we heard last night' (TLN 886), he is told that it was not Viola but Feste who sang the song. As it is odd that Orsino should confuse his beautiful servant with an old clown, and odd, too, that Feste should then appear and sing the song when he has no reason to be in Orsino's house (and is Olivia's fool), we seem to have here a palimpsestic text bearing traces of the fact that Viola was once a singer, now replaced in that capacity by

---

[201] The relevant Manningham passage is produced on Folger Shakespeare Library, 'Shakespeare Documented', https://shakespearedocumented.folger.edu/resource/document/john-manninghams-diary-earliest-mention-twelfth-night-and-shakespeare-anecdote [accessed 17 July 2022]; Taylor and Loughnane, 534–5.

Feste.[202] Given the musicality of the revision and the previous musicality of the underlying text, we might suspect that the version we have is a Blackfriars revision of an (Inns of) Court play, or a Blackfriars revision of a Blackfriars play, or an (Inns of) Court revision of a Blackfriars play. As the play was performed in the Banqueting House, Whitehall, on 6 April 1618, we might in fact wonder whether that is the text that has been preserved in the Folio.[203]

In other words, the period when *Twelfth Night* was originally written must indeed have preceded Manningham's 1602 reference, but the *Twelfth Night* that survives seems to bear internal hallmarks of being a later text. It should be added here too that having dated the play by its external information, we then treat as mistaken the idea that the text of the play that survives might have a later date. Yet, as Laurie E. Osborne perceptively observes, 'For the readers of the early nineteenth century, *Twelfth Night* is a comedy self-evidently from the close of Shakespeare's career. Yet, for the twentieth-century reader, with the benefit of 150 years of scholarship based on the 1601 date, *Twelfth Night* is obviously a middle comedy with connections to *Hamlet* and to the tragedies.'[204] The date – either date – in other words, apparently makes logical sense once it has been internalised as fact. The very notion that *Twelfth Night* is obviously a middle comedy, or a late one, is an interpretation that has come to seem factually rooted.

Then there is the date for *Julius Caesar*. Malone put it at 1607 in all three of his *Attempts*, a dating broadly accepted until, again, new external information changed that. Gustav Binz, in 1899, published '*Londoner Theater und Schauspiele im Jahr 1599*', alerting readers to an account he

---

[202] This point is regularly made by music historians and questioned by theatre historians. It is suggested by Peter J. Seng, *The Vocal Songs in the Plays of Shakespeare: A Critical History* (Cambridge, MA: Harvard University Press, 1967), 109; and Winifred Maynard, 'Ballads, Songs, and Masques in the Plays of Shakespeare', in her *Elizabethan Lyric Poetry and Its Music* (Oxford: Clarendon Press, 1986), 202.

[203] See Wiggins, '*Twelfth Night*', *British Drama: A Catalogue*, 4: 321.

[204] Laurie E. Osborne, 'Double Dating in *Twelfth Night*', in her *The Trick of Singularity: 'Twelfth Night' and the Performance Editions* (Iowa City: University of Iowa Press, 1996), 1–14.

had found by Thomas Platter the Younger, a Swiss diarist, about a visit to the Globe on 21 September 1599.[205] Translated, Platter's text reads: 'we saw the tragedy of the first emperor Julius Caesar, very pleasingly performed, with approximately fifteen characters; at the end of the play they danced together admirably and exceedingly gracefully, according to their custom, two in each group dressed in men's and two women's apparel.'[206]

Actually, this account, though almost certainly of a play at the Globe (suggestions that this is a Rose play can be rejected; the Rose was apparently shut at the time), need not be a reference to the Folio-only text of *Julius Caesar* that we have.[207] The Folio text that survives, which ends on preparations for a funeral, does not obviously call for a dance; that better fits the way that comedies end. Platter, moreover, does not seem to be recalling an unconnected clown's jig, for he describes a graceful and decorous company celebration. With so little detail, there is not much more to say except that we have, from the discovery of Platter's diary onwards, put the text we have in the 1599 slot when chronologically ordering editions, so that it is in sequence with *As You Like It* and *Henry V*.[208] Malone thought, from internal evidence, that the text dated to several years later and found natural company with what he believed to be Shakespeare's next play (also classical, also starring Antony and also sourced in North's Plutarch): *Antony and Cleopatra*. If we question the Platter account's relationship with the text we have, a different date range

---

[205] *Anglia* 22 (1899), 456–64. Binz' discovery is discussed and contextualised in M. L. Stapleton, 'Thomas Platter and Gustav Binz', https://users.pfw.edu /stapletm/NVSJC/Platter.html [accessed 17 July 2022].

[206] Translation by Ernest Schanzer, 'Thomas Platter's Observations on the Elizabethan Stage', *Notes & Queries* 201 (1956), 456–7.

[207] Taylor and Loughnane, 528.

[208] Taylor and Loughnane, 528, support the 1599 date, though the two stylometric scholars it quotes reach different conclusions: Marina Tarlinksaja, looking at strong metrical breaks, places the play between *Henry V* and *Troilus and Cressida*; MacDonald P. Jackson, looking at speech length places it between *Twelfth Night* and *Troilus and Cressida*. Both these conclusions, of course, are also dependent on agreeing 1602 is the date of the surviving *Troilus and Cressida* (first published in 1609).

once again becomes possible. As a play, *Caesar's Tragedy*, was performed at
court in 1613, as discussed in Section 2, we might at the least wonder
whether this is that version of the text, and, if so, whether its best sequential
order is with other plays of the late 1590s or late plays (or both).

Simon Forman's account of seeing four Globe plays in 1611 –
Shakespeare's *Macbeth*, *Winter's Tale* and *Cymbeline*, and a *Richard II* by
an unknown playwright – is only selectively used by us for dating: but that
is interesting too. Forman is quoted to confirm the dates of *Cymbeline* and
Winter's Tale (though sometimes, as he does not mention a statue, also used
to question the date of the statue scene) as 1610–11. But though Forman's
description of 'Mackbeth at the glod [Globe]' provides the earliest external
information we have about *Macbeth*, the account is, unusually, not used to
date that play – despite the fact that the musical *Witch* inserts also date the
play to around that time.[209] An argument could be made, from the Forman
account, for a later date for the *Macbeth* play. Instead, however, this
information participates in the different way in which Malone – and we –
treat what is perceived as 'early' and 'late' information: early confirms; 'late'
can be discounted. This is not necessarily to question the conclusion made
by all recent editions about the date of *Macbeth* but to show how the same
arguments and kinds of information used to date some plays are used to
reject others, and that it is intriguing how often evidence, when found,
frustrates the certainty of dating. External evidence seldom backs up internal evidence, and vice versa, hence the need for interpretation.

Current editors, deciding how to organise complete works or date single
volumes, have one more, bleak eighteenth-century inheritance, *about* more
than *from* Malone, but it deeply concerns him: the way that friendships, or
the reverse, shape the field. Each single volume or collected works has its
own specific editor and general editors who themselves have followers (and,
sometimes, detractors); then, as now, alliances and antagonisms shape the
field, and the conclusions they reach. In an 1802 letter Malone writes that

---

[209] Reproduced in Folger Shakespeare Library, 'Shakespeare Documented',
https://shakespearedocumented.folger.edu/resource/document/formans-
account-seeing-plays-globe-macbeth-cymbeline-winters-tale [accessed 17 July
2022].

'The persevering rancour and incessant malignity and animosity, with which Steevens ... endeavoured to carp at and depretiate *all* my notes, on which any sarcasm or cavil could be fastened, (even those which while I was only a *co-adjutor*, he received as highly valuable and unobjectionable,) is known probably only to myself.'[210] Steevens came to resent his one-time *protégé* Malone and expressed his thoughts shrilly and in print; his malevolence was, by the end of his life, such that he 'would annihilate even Shakespeare himself, that he might gain a triumph over Malone'.[211] Bullying, and *ad hominem* attacks, on online forums as well as in print, and often involving senior scholars and editors, continue to typify editorial disagreement about revision, adaptation, attribution and other issues that determine chronology. The least generous such attacks are, remarks Brandi Kristine Adams, 'the stuff of men' and employ 'the combative nature and rhetoric of war'. Who wrote, who revised, who rewrote the text – and when – are as a result the most male subfields of Shakespeare studies, despite the welcome improvements noted by Molly G. Yarn in her *Shakespeare's 'Lady Editors'*.[212] Personal attacks trivialise editing, scare new scholars and demote and sometimes demonise the author they are supposedly advancing: Shakespeare. At a time when the humanities, and the place of Shakespeare within them, are under threat, it behoves us all to protect our subject, and one another, better.

7 Conclusion

Given that we require chronologies to organise our thoughts about Shakespeare, how might we rethink them to avoid some of the challenges

[210] Letter of 5 June 1802, *The Correspondence of Thomas Percy and Edmond Malone*, ed. Arthur Tillotson (Baton Rouge, Louisiana: Louisiana State University Press, 1944), 93–4.

[211] Isaac Disraeli, *A Second Series of Curiosities of Literature, and The Literary Character Illustrated*, 3 vols (London: John Murray, 1824), 3: 46.

[212] Brandi Kristine Adams, 'Mediators of the Wor(l)d: Editors, Shakespeare and Inclusion', https://beforeshakespeare.com [accessed 17 July 2022]; Molly Yarn, *Shakespeare's 'Lady Editors'* (Cambridge: Cambridge University Press, 2021).

highlighted in this Element? First, I suggest that we redefine what it is we are looking for. The very notion of coming up with a single date for when a play was written is nebulous, as discussed – for the idea that Shakespeare firmly completed one play before embarking on another has here been questioned: there may be a great deal of overlap, not just between plays that – in our chronologies – are placed side by side but also between plays that are far apart; an earlier play may be being revised while a later one is being written. De Grazia succinctly summarises the problem: 'The hard fact is that we do not know when Shakespeare wrote his plays. We might know the date when a play was performed by the acting company or when it was published by the stationer, but neither date should be mistaken for the one we have most wanted: the date when it was written by Shakespeare.'[213]

As opposed to a question about an undefinable and often fluid event, it makes better sense to ask about something that happened on a fixed occasion. Impressively, *The New Oxford Shakespeare* has attempted to do this, and as well as a first volume of complete works modernised and printed in 'chronological order', and subject to internal/external issue to which that gives rise, it has second and third volumes in old spelling called the *Critical Reference Edition*. In those two volumes, plays are presented in the order in which they were first published: the first volume provides texts printed in Shakespeare's lifetime; the second texts printed after Shakespeare's death. Print order *is* largely knowable, with the exception of lost print runs (as for the first quarto of *Love's Labour's Lost*), so these two volumes provide a new way of thinking about chronology.[214] The disadvantage of choosing print order, however, is that it is not very yielding. It discloses the way an early modern reader might have encountered the published texts of Shakespeare, provided that that reader bought and read *all* of the texts in the order in which they came out; it is not very

---

[213] de Grazia, *Four Shakespearean*, 62.

[214] Discussed in David McInnis, 'We've found a Shakespeare Folio but a swag of original plays are still missing', for *The Conversation*, https://theconversation .com/weve-found-a-shakespeare-Folio-but-a-swag-of-original-plays-are-still- missing-54596 [accessed 17 July 2022].

revelatory about performance or authorship. And as eighteen of Shakespeare's plays were not published until they appeared all together in the Folio, so print order does not have much to say about nearly half of Shakespeare's texts.

A more obvious solution is to ask not 'when were plays first written?', but 'when were they first performed?' That shares, with the question of when they were written, the huge disadvantage that speculation is required to produce an answer. But it has two advantages. The first is that it is a question for which there actually is *an* answer, even if shrouded in the mists of time – there *was* a first performance – whereas the date of first writing has been shown to be a confused concept. The second is that, having definitely happened, a first performance also definitely occurred in a sequence before or after other first performances (while, as argued, two or more plays might have been being written, or revised and updated, at any one time). In practical terms, most external information – the 'diary' of Henslowe, the *Office Book* of Herbert, the surviving court records of production – are themselves records of performance, so a further advantage would be that such minimal information as we do have somewhat addresses this question. Indeed, though the title pages of Shakespeare's published texts or the SR licences reveal so little about 'writing' that they do not always name their author (and never, of course, mention place or time of composition), they do contain performance information such as the company responsible, the theatre where the play was performed and sometimes even the specific and dated occurrence of court performances.

The trouble with a performance list, however, is that it will have to be partial as well as speculative: locating plays for which there is no external information along a performance trajectory will be impossible. Indeed, the two plays for which we seem to have obvious first-performance dates are ambiguous: the Globe playhouse burnt down at what was said to be a first performance of *All Is True* but, as argued, Malone was only the first to have thought that to have been a revival performance of an earlier play; *1 Henry VI* was said to be 'ne' (which may mean 'new', though the word itself is obscure) in Henslowe's *Diary* – but that is a play whose very authorship, and relationship to Shakespeare, has always been in question: the reference could be to a different, non-Shakespearean, play entirely. A performance list, then, would provide only questionable information and only about some texts. That would ultimately be an advantage too, however, in that it would serve to 'unteach', reminding readers how hard chronological certainty is to come by and how little is conveyed by trustable external sources. The list could be called something like 'the work', to make clear that it is about the play of that name, not about the surviving text.

There would then need to be a second, flanking list, 'the text'. It would be on the extant text(s), considering issues of lateness and revision as well as adaptation. Every surviving text could be on that list – more than once if there is a quarto/octavo and Folio text – and all dates on the list would potentially be date ranges, reflecting the different (somewhat) datable passages found in the text (with the hefty proviso that dating from a vague word or historical event is itself contentious, and that all the dates on the list are therefore open to question). The fact that that list would be relatively different from the external list, as well as broader in remit, would again work as a caveat, reminding readers that most plays are palimpsests containing additions and revisions from different periods of time; that a date range may include references to dates from before the time the text was complete, or after Shakespeare died; and that there is a lot that we don't know – and can never know. It is suggested, further, that 'early' information be separated from 'late' information, and 'external' from 'internal'.

The rangy chronology and its mixed performance/(re)writing information would, of course, be unwieldy, and we would lose the crispness that has come with the single chronology. But, as suggested in this Element, the single chronology that has dictated our method of thinking about Shakespeare for so long has brought about conclusions and sequences that may not be there. Thus a section might, in incapsulated form, look something like Table 2, showing the differing information and supplying the source for it (in this instance stylometric information is taken from Taylor and Loughnane; and later external information is taken from Wiggins's *Catalogue*).

This Element on Malone has shown how great and how flawed the immense scholarship of that erudite and careful man was, and how his authority was such that even when individual datings of his have been challenged and changed, his method has not. Moreover, we do not always

Table 2 Chronological possibilities External = sure; Internal = questionable

Name	The Work	The Text	'Earliness'	'Lateness'
Othello: Q	1604	1604–6	External: 1604 Court Perf; blasphemy (so pre-1606 Act) Internal: Macdonald P. Jackson [closest to *Hamlet*]; Helmut Ilsemann [between *Measure* and *Lear*]; metrical breaks [after *Hamlet* before *Measure*]	Internal: Absence Willow song pre-pared for in text: shows cutting?
Othello: F	1604	1606–22	External: Swearing reduced (post-1606); 1610 Globe and Oxford perf; 1612–13 court perfs Internal: As above	External: Errant SDs show Crane's 1620s additions Internal: Presence Willow song (suggs court/Blackfriars)?

Table 2 (cont.)

Name	The Work	The Text	'Earliness'	'Lateness'
Twelfth Night: F	1599–1602	1608?+	External: Middle Temple perf 1602 Internal: MacDonald P. Jackson [text closest to *Othello*]; Ants Oras [text closest to *Hamlet*]	External: Performed in Banqueting House, Whitehall 1618 Internal: Apparently revised text (songs changed from Viola to Feste); music suggests Blackfriars/ court

remember his careful caveat that all chronology is uncertain: instead, over time, his conjectures, added to ours, have solidified into seeming facts; accumulated information, even if not fully persuasive when separately looked at, has seemed to provide proof of concept. The ramifications have been far-reaching. As shown, chronology instantly became biography, providing a sequence for Shakespeare's plays that could be read against his life: from Malone's time onwards, all biographies of Shakespeare have traced his psychological and intellectual development (as well as, sometimes, events in his life) quoting the texts that survive as though in chronological sequence. For a linked reason, complete works have sometimes printed plays in 'chronological' order, supposedly showing Shakespeare's development over time, though not his rethinking over time, which might have put the same texts in a different order. Chronology affects theatre history, too, by seemingly determining, in ways questioned here, which text was played in which theatre (Theatre/ Globe/Blackfriars), by which company, and under which monarch. Chronology likewise affects bibliography, by suggesting, for instance, the amount of time that separates performance from print. For stylometric analyses chronology is crucial, as it supplies information about which 'clusters' were written around the same time, or which texts preceded or succeeded one another. Chronology has, finally, come to affect our sense of Shakespeare and periodisation, which determines how plays are taught and books are written: 'early Shakespeare' and 'late Shakespeare', or 'Elizabethan Shakespeare' and 'Jacobean Shakespeare', are concepts that have been produced by chronological means.

It was Malone's authority, his carefully presented sources, his balanced and cautious approach to them and his large gathered field of evidence that resulted in his seeming 'correct' in his method, and to those who countered him seeming perverse, wayward, fanciful, poetic.[215] Questioning his correctness, while paying homage to his brilliance, enables us to interrogate not just our own chronologies – so deeply bound up with his – but also the conclusions reached in the many other fields that are chronologically dependent on them.

[215] Martin, xvii.

'Instability' has long been an exciting byword for the contingent nature of Shakespeare's texts: 'malleable', 'flexible', 'multiplicitous' and 'adaptive' have all been used to counter the weighty and deadening tradition that for so long gave a rigid – and mistaken – fixity to the texts. But the corollary has not been followed through. If the texts are unstable, then so are their chronologies. In exploring chronological instability, revealed and hidden by Malone in the process of inventing a chronological methodology, it is hoped that this Element offers the excitement, as well as the confusion, that a lack of certainty provides. In raising questions even about Malone's measured conjectures, it hopes to offer instead the exhilaration and the possibilities that come with rethinking, from first principles, a subject that is so much more exciting and complex (because so much less secure) than was once thought.

References

Publisher and location are supplied for all texts after 1800; for pre-1800 texts, location is London unless otherwise stated.

Adams, Brandi Kristine, 'Mediators of the Wor(l)d: Editors, Shakespeare and Inclusion', https://beforeshakespeare.com [accessed 17 July 2022].

Anon, 'Notes and Various Readings of Shakespeare', *The Critical Review* 56, ed. Tobias Smollett (1783), 401–9.

Anon, 'The Plays and Poems of William Shakspeare', *The Critical Review* 3, ed. Tobias Smollett (1791), 361–9.

Anon, 'The Plays of William Shakspeare', *Monthly Review* 62 (1780), 12–26.

Anupam Basu and Joseph Loewenstein, with Douglas Knox, John Ladd and Stephen Pentecost, 'EarlyPrint Library', https://ada.artsci.wustl.edu/corpus-frontend-1.2/eebotcp/search/ [accessed 17 July 2022].

Arber, Edward, ed., *A Transcript of the Registers of the Company of Stationers of London*, 5 vols (London: Privately printed, 1875–84).

Barroll, J. Leeds, *Politics, Plague and Shakespeare's Theatre* (London: Cornell University Press, 1991).

Bate, Jonathan and Eric Rasmussen, eds., *William Shakespeare: Complete Works* (2nd ed., London: Bloomsbury Academic, 2022).

Bawcutt, N. W., ed., *The Control and Censorship of Caroline Drama: The Records of Sir Henry Herbert, Master of the Revels, 1623–73* (Oxford: Oxford University Press, 1996).

Bawcutt, N. W., ed., *Malone Society: Collections, 15* (Manchester: Manchester University Press, 1994).

Beaumont, Francis, and John Fletcher, *Comedies and Tragedies* (1647).

Bevington, David, ed., *The Complete Works of Shakespeare* (4th ed., New York: Longman, 1997).

Biddle, Martin, 'The Gardens of Nonsuch', *Garden History* 27 (1999), 145–83.

Binz, Gustav, '*Londoner Theater und Schauspiele im Jahr 1599*', *Anglia* 22 (1899), 456–64.

Blayney, Peter, 'The Publication of Playbooks', in *A New History of Early English Drama*, ed. John D. Cox and David Scott Kastan (New York: Columbia Press, 1997), 383–422.

Boswell, James, *A Biographical Memoir of the Late Edmond Malone, Esq* (London: Nichols, Son, and Bentley, 1813).

Bourus, Terri, *Young Shakespeare's Young Hamlet* (New York: Palgrave, 2014).

Bowles, Amy, 'Dressing the Text: Ralph Crane's Scribal Publication of Drama', *The Review of English Studies* 67 (2016), 405–27.

Brome, Richard, *Five New Playes* (1659).

Browne, William, *The Shepheards Pipe* (1614).

Capell, Edward, *Notes and Various Readings to Shakespeare*, 3 vols (1779–80).

Carpenter, Nan Cooke, 'Shakespeare and Music: Unexplored Areas', in *Shakespeare and the Arts*, ed. Stephen Orgel and Sean Keilen (New York: Garland, 1999), 123–35.

Chambers, E. K., *Shakespeare: A Study of Facts and Problems*, 2 vols (Oxford: Clarendon Press, 1930).

Chan, Mary, *Music in the Theatre of Ben Jonson* (Oxford: Clarendon Press, 1980).

Clarke, Andrea, and Karen Limper-Herz, 'The Making of the Tombs', https://blogs.bl.uk/digitisedmanuscripts/2022/02/the-making-of-the-tombs.html [accessed 17 July 2022].

Coleridge, Samuel Taylor, *The Notebooks*, ed. Kathleen Coburn, 5 vols in 10 (New York: Pantheon Books, 1973).

Coleridge, Samuel Taylor, *Shakespeare Criticism: Marginalia, Lectures, and other Notes from Coleridge's Manuscripts*, ed. Thomas Middleton Raysor, 2 vols (London: Constable, 1930).

Collier, J. Payne, *The History of English Dramatic Poetry to the Time of Shakespeare and the Annals of the Stage to the Restoration*, 3 vols (London: John Murray, 1831).

Cooper, Thomas, *The Wonderfull Mysterie* (1622).

Cunningham, Peter, *Extracts from the Accounts of the Revels at Court* (London: The Shakespeare Society, 1842).

Cutts, John P., 'New Findings with Regard to the 1624 Protection List', *Shakespeare Survey* 19 (1967), 101–7.

Cutts, John P., 'The Original Music to Middleton's *The Witch*', *Shakespeare Quarterly* 7 (1956), 203–9.

Daniel, Samuel, *Delia and Rosamond Augmented* (1594).

de Grazia, Margreta, *Four Shakespearean Period Pieces* (Chicago: University of Chicago Press, 2021).

de Grazia, Margreta, *Shakespeare Verbatim* (Oxford: Clarendon Press, 1991).

Disraeli, Isaac, *A Second Series of Curiosities of Literature, and The Literary Character Illustrated*, 3 vols (London: John Murray, 1824).

Dutton, Richard, *Shakespeare, Court Dramatist* (Oxford: Oxford University Press, 2016).

Dutton, Richard, *Shakespeare's Theatre: A History* (Hoboken: Wiley Blackwell, 2018).

Erne, Lukas, *Shakespeare as Literary Dramatist* (Cambridge: Cambridge University Press, 2003).

Fletcher, John, and Philip Massinger, *The Bloody Brother* (1639).

Fletcher, John, and William Shakespeare, *The Two Noble Kinsmen* (1634).

Folger Shakespeare Library, The, *'Shakespeare Documented'*, https://shakespearedocumented.folger.edu/ [accessed 17 July 2022].

Freeman, Arthur, and Janet Ing Freeman, *John Payne Collier: Scholarship and Forgery in the Nineteenth Century*, 2 vols (New Haven: Yale University Press, 2004).

Gadd, Ian, 'The Use and Misuse of *Early English Books Online*', *Literature Compass* 6 (2009), 680–92.

Green, Keith, 'John Wilson's Music for Richard Brome's The Northern Lass', *Early Modern Literary Studies*, 20 (2018). https://extra.shu.ac.uk/emls/journal/index.php/emls/article/view/281/317 [accessed 20 Jan 2023].

Greenblatt, Stephen, Walter Cohen, Suzanne Gossett, Jean E. Howard, Katherine' Eisaman Maus and Gordon McMullan, *The Norton Shakespeare*, 3rd ed. (New York: Norton, 2016).

Greene, Robert, *Greenes, Groats-worth of Witte* (1592).

Greene, Robert, *Menaphon* (1589).

Gurr, Andrew, *The Shakespeare Company* (Cambridge: Cambridge University Press, 2004).

H., S., *Sicily and Naples* (1640).

Halliwell-Phillipps, J. O., *Outlines of the Life of Shakespeare*, 2 vols (London: Longmans, Green, & Co., 1887).

Halmi, Nicholas, ed., *Wordsworth's Poetry and Prose* (New York: Norton, 2016).

Hattaway, Michael, *New Cambridge Shakespeare: As You Like It* (Cambridge: Cambridge University Press, 2000).

Hirsh, James, 'Act Divisions in the Shakespeare First Folio', *Papers of the Bibliographical Society of America* 96 (2002), 219–56.

Hosley, Richard, 'Was there a Music-Room in Shakespeare's Globe', *Shakespeare Survey* 13 (1960), 113–23.

Howard-Hill, T. H., *Ralph Crane and Some Shakespeare First Folio Comedies* (Charlottesville: University of Virginia Bibliographical Society, 1972).

Howard-Hill, T. H., 'Shakespeare's Earliest Editor, Ralph Crane', *Shakespeare Survey* 44 (1992), 113–30.

John Chamberlain, *Letters*, ed. Norman E. McClure, 2 vols (Philadelphia: American Philosophical Society, 1939).

Johnson, Samuel, ed., *The Plays of William Shakespeare*, 8 vols (1765).

Johnson, Samuel and George Steevens, eds., *The Plays of William Shakespeare*, 10 vols (1778).

Jonson, Ben, *The Comicall Satyre of Every Man out of his Humor* (1600).

Kerrigan, John, 'Revision, Adaptation, and the Fool in King Lear', in *The Division of the Kingdoms: Shakespeare's Two Versions of 'King Lear'* ed. Gary Taylor and Michael Warren (Oxford: Clarendon Press, 1983), 195–239.

Kiséry, András, 'Companionate Publishing, Literary Publics, and the Wit of Epyllia: The Early Success of *Hero and Leander*', in *Christopher Marlowe, Theatrical Commerce and the Book Trade*, ed. Kirk Melnikoff and Roslyn Knutson (Cambridge: Cambridge University Press, 2018), 165–81.

Lesser, Zachary, *'Hamlet' After Q1: An Uncanny History of the Shakespearean Text* (Philadelphia: University of Philadelphia Press, 2014).

Lindley, David, 'Music and Shakespearean Revision', *Archiv* 249 (2012), 50–64.

Lodge, Thomas, *Wits Miserie* (1596).

Lupić, Ivan, 'Shakespeare, Cardenio, and the Vertue Manuscripts', *Ars & Humanitas* 5 (2010), 74–91.

Malone, Edmond, *An Attempt to Ascertain the Order in which the Plays Attributed to Shakspeare were Written* in William Shakespeare, *The Plays*, ed. Samuel Johnson and George Steevens, 10 vols (1778).

Malone, Edmond, *An Attempt* to Ascertain the Order in which the Plays Attributed to Shakspeare were Written in William Shakespeare, *The Plays and Poems*, ed. Edmond Malone, 10 vols (1790).

Malone, Edmond, *An Attempt to Ascertain the Order in which the Plays Attributed to Shakespeare were Written* in William Shakespeare, *Plays and Poems*, ed. James Boswell and Edmond Malone, 21 vols (London: F. C. and J. Rivington et al., 1821).

Malone, Edmond, *An Historical Account of the Rise and Progress of the English Stage* (Basil: J. J. Tourneisen, 1800).

Malone, Edmond, ed., *The Plays and Poems of William Shakspeare*, 10 vols (1790).

Malone, Edmond and James Boswell, eds., *The Plays and Poems of William Shakspeare*, 21 vols (London: F. C. and J. Rivington et al., 1821).

Markham, Gervase, *The True Tragedy of Herod and Antipater* (1622).

Marino, James J., 'The Anachronistic Shrews', *Shakespeare Quarterly*, 60 (2009), 25–46.

Marston, John, *Antonio and Mellida* (1602).

Marston, John, *The Malcontent* [. . .] *With the Additions* [. . .] *by John Webster* (1604).

Martin, Peter, *Edmond Malone, Shakespearean Scholar*, 2nd ed. (Cambridge: Cambridge University Press, 1995).

Masten, Jeffrey, *Textual Intercourse* (Cambridge: Cambridge University Press, 1997).

Maynard, Winifred, 'Ballads, Songs, and Masques in the Plays of Shakespeare', in *Elizabethan Lyric Poetry and Its Music* (Oxford: Clarendon Press, 1986), 151–223.

McInnis, David, *Shakespeare and Lost Plays* (Cambridge: Cambridge University Press, 2021).

McInnis, David, 'We've found a Shakespeare Folio but a Swag of Original Plays are Still Missing', for *The Conversation*, https://theconversation .com/weve-found-a-shakespeare-Folio-but-a-swag-of-original-plays-are-still-missing-54596 [accessed 17 July 2022].

McMillin, Scott, ed., *The First Quarto of Othello* (Cambridge: Cambridge University Press, 2001).

McMullan, Gordon, *Shakespeare and the Idea of Late Writing: Authorship in the Proximity of Death* (Cambridge: Cambridge University Press, 2007).

Meres, Francis, *Palladis Tamia* (1598).

Middleton, Thomas, *The Ant, and the Nightingale: Or Father Hubburds Tales* (1604)

Middleton, Thomas, *The Witch*, ed. L. Drees and Henry de Vocht (Louvain: Librairie Universitaire, 1945).

Middleton, Thomas, *The Witch*, ed. W. W. Greg and F. P. Wilson (Oxford: Oxford University Press, the Malone Society Reprints, 1948).

Morus Londinium, 'Timeline of the Mulberry Tree in London', https://www.moruslondinium.org/research/timeline [accessed 17 July 2022].

Mowat, Barbara, 'Q2 *Othello* and the 1606 "Acte to Restrain the Abuses of Players"', in *Varianten – Variants – Variantes*, ed. Christa Jansohn and Bodo Planchta (Tübingen: Max Niemeyer, 2005), 91–106.

Munro, J., ed., *The Shakspere Allusion Book*, 2 vols (London: Chatto and Windus, 1909).

Neill, Michael ed., *The Oxford Shakespeare: Othello* (Oxford: Oxford University Press, 2006).

Orlin, Lena Cowen, *The Private Life of William Shakespeare* (Oxford: Oxford University Press, 2021).

Osborne, Laurie E., 'Double Dating in *Twelfth Night*', in *The Trick of Singularity: 'Twelfth Night' and the Performance Edition*s (Iowa City: University of Iowa Press, 1996), 1–18.

Palfrey, Simon and Tiffany Stern, *Shakespeare in Parts* (Oxford: Oxford University Press, 2009).

Playford, John, *Select Musicall Ayres, and Dialogues, For One and Two Voyces, to Sing to the Theorbo, Lute, or Basse Violl* (1652).

Pope, Alexander, ed., *The Works of Mr. William Shakespear*, 6 vols (1725).

Power, Andrew J., and Rory Loughnane eds, *Late Shakespeare, 1608-1613* (Cambridge: Cambridge University Press, 2012).

Prior, James, *Life of Edmond Malone* (London: Smith, Elder, and Co., 1860).

Rowe, Nicholas, ed., *The Works of Mr. William Shakespear*, 6 vols (1709).

Sabol, Andrew J., *Four Hundred Songs and Dances form the Stuart Masque* (Providence, RI: Brown University Press, 1978).

Sabol, Andrew J., *Songs and Dances for the Stuart Masque* (Providence, RI: Brown University Press, 1959).

Schoenbaum, S., *Internal Evidence and Elizabethan Dramatic Authorship* (London: Arnold, 1966).

Schoenbaum, S., *Shakespeare's Lives* (Oxford: Clarendon Press, 1971).

Schanzer, Ernest, 'Thomas Platter's Observations on the Elizabethan Stage', *Notes & Queries* 201 (1956), 456–7.

Schiffer, James, 'Taking the Long View: *Twelfth Night* Criticism and Performance', in *Twelfth Night: New Critical Essays*, ed. James Schiffer (London: Routledge, 2011), 1–44.

Schoch, Richard W., 'Edmond Malone and the Search for Theatrical Intelligence', in *Writing the History of the British Stage, 1660-1900* (Cambridge: Cambridge University Press, 2018), 255–93.

Seng, Peter J., *The Vocal Songs in the Plays of Shakespeare; a Critical History* (Cambridge, MA: Harvard University Press, 1967).

Shakespeare, William, *A Most Pleasaunt and Excellent Conceited Comedie, of Syr Iohn Falstaffe, and the Merrie Wiues of Windsor* (1602).

Shakespeare, William, *Mr William Shakespeares Comedies, Histories, & Tragedies* ['The First Folio'] (1623) in Norton Facsimile, prepared by Charlton Hinman (New York: Norton, 1968).

Shakespeare, William, *Poems* (1640).

Sherbo, Arthur, *Shakespeare's Midwives: Some Neglected Shakespeareans* (Delaware: University of Delaware Press, 1992).

Smith, Irwin, *Shakespeare's Blackfriars Playhouse* (New York: New York University Press, 1964).

Stapleton, M. L., 'Thomas Platter and Gustav Binz', https://users.pfw.edu/stapletm/NVSJC/Platter.html [accessed 17 July 2022].

Stern, Tiffany, *Documents of Performance* (Oxford: Oxford University Press, 2009).

Stern, Tiffany, 'Inventing Stage Directions; Demoting Dumb Shows', in *Stage Directions and Shakespearean Theatre*, ed. Sarah Dustagheer and Gillian Woods for Arden Shakespeare (London: Bloomsbury 2017), 19–43.

Stern, Tiffany, *Rehearsal from Shakespeare to Sheridan* (Oxford: Oxford University Press, 2000).

Stern, Tiffany, 'A Ruinous Monastery: The Second Blackfriars as a Place of Nostalgia', in *Moving Shakespeare Indoors*, ed. Andrew Gurr and Farah Karim-Cooper (Cambridge: Cambridge University Press, 2014), 97–114.

Stern, Tiffany, 'Stage Directions', in *Book Parts*, ed. Dennis Duncan and Adam Smyth (Oxford: Oxford University Press, 2019).

Sternfeld, Frederick William, *Music in Shakespearean Tragedy* (London: Routledge and Kegan Paul, 1962).

Stopes, C. C., *The Seventeenth Century Accounts of the Masters of the Revels* (London: Oxford University Press, 1922).

Stow, John, *A Suruay of London* (1598).

Symonds, E. M., 'The Diary of John Greene (1634-57)', *English Historical Review* 43 (1928), 385–94

Tannenbaum, S. A., *Shakespeare Forgeries in the Revels Accounts* (New York: Columbia University Press, 1928).

Taylor, Gary, and Rory Loughnane, 'The Canon and Chronology of Shakespeare's Works', in *The New Oxford Shakespeare: Authorship Companion* ed. Gary Taylor and Gabriel Egan (Oxford: Oxford University Press, 2017), 417–603.

Taylor, Gary, and Gabriel Egan eds., *The New Oxford Shakespeare: Authorship Companion* (Oxford: Oxford University Press, 2017).

Gary Taylor, John Jowett, Terri Bourus and Gabriel Egan, *The New Oxford Shakespeare: The Complete Works* (Oxford: Oxford University Press, 2016).

Taylor, Gary, and John Jowett, *Shakespeare Reshaped* (Oxford: Clarendon Press, 1993).

Taylor, Gary, 'The Structure of Performance: Act-Intervals in the London Theatres, 1576-1642', in *Shakespeare Reshaped 1606-1623*, ed. Gary Taylor and John Jowett (Oxford: Oxford University Press, 1993), 3–50.

Text Creation Partnership, The, 'About EEBO-TCP' https://textcreationpartnership.org/tcp-texts/eebo-tcp-early-english-books-online/ [accessed 17 July 2022].

Tillotson, Arthur, ed., *Correspondence of Thomas Percy and Edmond Malone* (Baton Rouge, Louisiana: Louisiana State University Press, 1944).

Tyrwhitt, Thomas, *Observations and Conjectures upon some Passages of Shakespeare* (1766).

Walls, Peter, *Music in the English Courtly Masque, 1604-1640* (Oxford: Oxford University Press, 1996).

Wiggins, Martin, in association with Catherine Richardson, *British Drama: a Catalogue*, 9 vols to date (Oxford: Oxford University Press, 2015).

Walsh, Marcus, 'George Steevens and the 1778 Variorum: a Hermeneutics and a Social Economy of Annotation', in *Shakespeare and the Eighteenth Century*, ed. Peter Sabor and Paul Yachnin (Aldershot: Ashgate, 2008), 155–66.

W[arner], W[illiam], *Menaecmi* (1595).

Weis, René, ed., *Arden Shakespeare: Romeo and Juliet* (London: Bloomsbury, 2012).

Werstine, Paul, *Early Modern Playhouse Manuscripts and the Editing of Shakespeare* (Cambridge: Cambridge University Press, 2013).

Wright, James, *Historia Histrionica* (1699).

Yarn, Molly, *Shakespeare's 'Lady Editors'* (Cambridge: Cambridge University Press, 2021).

Shakespeare and Text

Claire M. L. Bourne
The Pennsylvania State University

Claire M. L. Bourne is Assistant Professor of English at the Pennsylvania State University. She is author of *Typographies of Performance in Early Modern England* (2020) and editor of the collection *Shakespeare/Text* (2021). She has published extensively on early modern book design and reading practices in venues such as *PBSA*, *ELR*, *Shakespeare* and numerous edited collections. She is also co-author (with Jason Scott-Warren) of an article attributing the annotations in the Free Library of Philadelphia's copy of the Shakespeare First Folio to John Milton. She has edited Fletcher and Massinger's *The Sea Voyage* for the *Routledge Anthology of Early Modern Drama* (ed. Jeremy Lopez) and is working on an edition of *Henry the Sixth, Part 1* for the Arden Shakespeare, Fourth Series.

Rory Loughnane
University of Kent

Rory Loughnane is Reader in Early Modern Studies and Co-Director of the Centre for Medieval and Early Modern Studies at the University of Kent. He is the author or editor of nine books and has published widely on Shakespeare and textual studies. In his role as Associate Editor of the *New Oxford* Shakespeare, he has edited more than ten of Shakespeare's plays, and co-authored with Gary Taylor a book-length study about the 'Canon and Chronology' of Shakespeare's works. He is a General Editor of the forthcoming

About the Series
Cambridge Elements in Shakespeare and Text offers a platform for original scholarship about the creation, circulation, reception, remaking, use, performance, teaching, and translation of the Shakespearean text across time and place. The series seeks to publish research that challenges – and pushes beyond – the conventional parameters of Shakespeare and textual studies.

Cambridge Elements ⚌

Shakespeare and Text